Constance Wachtmeister

Reminiscences of H. P. Blavatsky and the Secret Doctrine

Constance Wachtmeister

Reminiscences of H. P. Blavatsky and the Secret Doctrine

ISBN/EAN: 9783743393271

Manufactured in Europe, USA, Canada, Australia, Japa

Cover: Foto ©Lupo / pixelio.de

Manufactured and distributed by brebook publishing software (www.brebook.com)

Constance Wachtmeister

Reminiscences of H. P. Blavatsky and the Secret Doctrine

REMINISCENCES

OF

H. P. BLAVATSKY

AND

"THE SECRET DOCTRINE"

BY

THE COUNTESS CONSTANCE WACHTMEISTER, F.T.S.

AND OTHERS

EDITED BY

A FELLOW OF THE THEOSOPHICAL SOCIETY

LONDON:
THEOSOPHICAL PUBLISHING SOCIETY,
7, DUKE STREET, ADELPHI, LONDON, W.C.
NEW YORK: *The Path*, 144, Madison Avenue.
MADRAS: Theosophical Society, Adyar.
1893
(All rights reserved.)

PREFACE.

This book has been written by several persons who had the advantage of being the most closely connected with Madame Blavatsky during her residence in Europe, while she was engaged in the great work of her life—"The Secret Doctrine."

It would be a difficult task to give full, detailed accounts of all the circumstances which occurred during the preparation of this remarkable work, because it must never be forgotten that H.P.B. was, as she often herself expressed it, only the compiler of the work. Behind her stood the real teachers, the guardians of the Secret Wisdom of the Ages, who taught her all the occult lore that she transmitted in writing. Her merit consisted partly in being able to assimilate the transcendental knowledge which was given out, in being a worthy messenger of her Masters, partly in her marvellous capability of rendering abstruse Eastern metaphysical thought in a form intelligible to Western minds, verifying and comparing Eastern Wisdom with Western Science. Much credit, also, is due to her for her great moral courage in representing to the world thoughts and theories wholly at variance with the materialistic Science of the present day. It will be understood with difficulty by many, that the much abused "phenomena" played an important part in the compilation of "The Secret Doctrine;" that H.P.B. very often received so-called precipitated messages, containing matter which later on became part of the book.

As the world gains better comprehension of occult laws, many strange events will be understood, and the history of the Theosophical Society will be viewed in another light than that in which hitherto it has been seen. During the last ten years, since the

"*Memoirs of H.P.B.*," by Mr. Sinnett, were published, a remarkable change has been growing in the leading minds of the West in their attitude towards occultism. Theories and facts which before were held up to scorn, are now considered worthy of investigation—such as transference of thought, consciousness after death, etc.—and therefore it may be hoped that the facts related in this book will meet with the fairness of judgment that any **bonâ fide** *account has the right to demand.*

Very cordial thanks are due to the friend—who wishes his name to remain unknown—who undertook the labour of editing the various accounts, and of arranging the, at first, somewhat chaotic material. The book would have gained in symmetry had all these accounts been thrown into a single consecutive story, but it has been thought better to leave each its own individual form, so as to retain the vivid impress of the conviction of each separate witness.

CONSTANCE WACHTMEISTER.

H. P. BLAVATSKY

AND

"THE SECRET DOCTRINE."

CHAPTER I.

IN giving an account of the manner in which *The Secret Doctrine* was written by H. P. Blavatsky, while yet the circumstances are fresh in my memory, with memoranda and letters still available for reference, I shall not shrink from dwelling at some length on my own relations with my dear friend and teacher, and on many attendant circumstances which, while not directly connected with the actual writing of the book, will contribute, I feel sure, to an intelligent comprehension of both the author and her work.

For me nothing is trivial, nothing meaningless, in the personality, in the habits, and in the environments f H.P.B., and I desire to convey to the reader, if possible, as full a knowledge as I myself possess of the difficulties and distractions that beset her during the progress of her work. The ill-health, the wandering life, the unpropitious surroundings, the lack of materials, the defection of false friends, the attacks of enemies, were obstacles that impeded her labour; but the co-operation of willing hands, the love and care of devoted adherents, and, above all, the support and direction of her beloved and revered Masters, rendered its completion possible.

It was in the year 1884 that, having occasion to visit London, I first made acquaintance with Helena Petrovna Blavatsky, at Mr. and Mrs. Sinnett's house. I well remember the feeling of pleasurable excitement with which I made that memorable call. I had previously read *Isis Unveiled* with wonder and admiration for the vast stores of strange knowledge contained in that remarkable work, therefore I was prepared to regard with feelings little short of reverence one who not only had founded a Society which promised to form the nucleus of a universal Brotherhood of Humanity, but who was also declared to be the messenger of men who had advanced beyond average mankind in mental and spiritual attainments, and thus could, in the truest sense, be called the Pioneers of our Race.

My reception by my hostess was cordial, and I was at once introduced to Madame Blavatsky. Her features were instinct with power, and expressed an innate nobility of character that more'than fulfilled the anticipations I had formed; but what chiefly arrested my attention was the steady gaze of her wonderful grey eyes, piercing yet calm and inscrutable: they shone with a serene light which seemed to penetrate and unveil the secrets of the heart.

When, however, I turned to look upon those who surrounded her, I experienced a revulsion of feeling that for a time left an uneasy impression on my mind. It was a strange scene that met my view. On the floor, at the foot of the low ottoman on which Madame Blavatsky was seated, several visitors were grouped who gazed up at her with an expression of homage and adoration, others hung upon her words with a studied show of rapt attention, and all seemed to me more or less affected by a prevailing tone of flattery.

As I sat apart and looked on at what was passing before me, I permitted suspicions, which I have since learned to be perfectly groundless and gratuitous, to rest in my mind. I trembled lest I should find that a character of which I had formed such elevated expectations should prove to be a slave of flattery and greedy of the adulation of her followers. I could not know at that time the aloofness, the indifference to praise or blame, the high sense of duty, not to be shaken by any selfish considerations, of the woman before me. I could not then tell that her nature was inherently incapable of degrading its powers and its great mission to the purchase of a cheap popularity.

Though too proud to justify herself to those who were incapable of appreciating the lofty standard of conduct which she followed herself and ever held up to the world in her ethical and mystic writings, she would occasionally open out her inner mind to those few earnest pupils who were pledged to tread the path she indicated. I have in recollection an explanation she gave, on this very point, when the crowd of scoffers in the press and in drawing-rooms asked one another: " How is it that this pupil of semi-omniscient Mahatmas, this natural clairvoyant and trained reader of the minds of men, cannot even tell her friends from her foes?"

" Who am I," she said, answering one question with another, " who am I that I should deny a chance to one in whom I see a spark still glimmering of recognition of the Cause I serve that might yet be fanned into a flame of devotion? What matter the consequences that fall on me personally when such an one fails, succumbing to the forces of evil within him—deception, ingratitude, revenge, what not—forces that I saw as clearly as I saw the hopeful spark: though in his fall he cover me with misrepresentation, obloquy and scorn? What right have I to refuse to any one the chance of profiting by the truths I can teach him, and thereby entering upon the Path? I tell you that I have no choice. I am pledged by the strictest rules and laws of occultism to a renunciation of selfish considerations, and how can I dare to assume the existence of faults in a candidate and act upon my assumption even though a cloudy forbidding aura may fill me with misgivings?"

CHAPTER II.

HERE I may perhaps allude briefly to the circumstances which led up to the visit to Madame Blavatsky that I have described. For two years, from 1879 to 1881, I had been investigating Spiritualism, with the result that, while I was forced into acceptance of the facts observed, I was wholly unable to accept the current Spiritualistic interpretation of those facts.

Towards the end of this time I met with *Isis Unveiled*, *Esoteric Buddhism*, and other Theosophical books, and finding the theories that I had formed independently in regard to the nature and cause of Spiritualistic phenomena corroborated and expanded in these works, I very naturally felt attracted towards Theosophy.

In 1881 I joined the ranks of the Theosophical Society and became affiliated to a Lodge.

The result of my studies here was, from various causes, unsatisfactory, and I returned to a course of private reading and research. Thus I was in sympathy with some aspects of Theosophic teaching and with subjects of which H.P.B. had made close study. The perusal of these books served to increase my admiration for Madame Blavatsky, so that when an opportunity occurred to make her acquaintance I seized upon it with alacrity.

Shortly after the visit mentioned I was present at an evening party at Mrs. Sinnett's, and there first met Colonel Olcott. His conversation, which drew around him a group of interested listeners, was directed chiefly to topics of "phenomena," and the strange experiences which had come under his own observation, or in which he had borne a part. All this, however, did not suffice to divert my attention from Madame Blavatsky, whose striking personality, and the mystery surrounding her life, fascinated me. Yet I did not approach her, but spent a pleasant evening apart with another new acquaintance, Madame Gebhard, who was later to become a very dear friend, and who entertained me with many stories of " the Old Lady," as H. P. B. was then familiarly called by her intimates.

These were the only occasions during my visit to London on which I saw H.P.B. and I had no expectation of meeting her again. I was making preparations for my departure, when one evening, to my great surprise, I received a letter addressed to me in an unfamiliar handwriting, which proved to be from Madame Blavatsky. This letter contained an invitation to come and see her in Paris, as she was anxious to have some private talk with me. The temptation to know more of one whose personality interested me so profoundly, and who was the founder of the society to which I belonged, prevailed with me, and I determined to return to Sweden *via* Paris.

On my arrival in Paris I called at Madame Blavatsky's *appartement*, but I was told that she was at Enghien on a visit to the Comtesse d'Adhémar. Nothing daunted, I took the train, and soon found myself in front of the pretty country seat of the d'Adhémars. Here fresh difficulties awaited me. On sending up my card with a request to see Madame Blavatsky, I was told, after some slight delay, that the lady was occupied and could not receive me. I replied that I was perfectly willing to wait, but having come from England at Madame Blavatsky's desire to see her, I declined to go away until my errand was perfor

Upon this I was shown into a salon full of people and the Comtesse d'Adhémar came forward, received me kindly, and led me to the other end of the room, where Madame Blavatsky was seated. After greetings and explanations, she told me she was to dine that evening in Paris with the Duchesse de Pomar, and asked me if I would accompany her. As the Duchesse was an old friend of my own who had always been most hospitable and kind, I felt assured she would not think me intrusive, so naturally I consented. The afternoon passed pleasantly in conversation with many interesting people and in listening to Madame Blavatsky's animated talk. In French her conversation was much more fluent than in English, and here even more than in London she was always the centre of a group of eager listeners.

In the carriage between Enghien and Paris H.P.B. was silent and *distraite*. She confessed to being tired, and we spoke but little, and upon the most commonplace subjects. Once, after a long pause, she told me that she distinctly heard the music of "Guillaume Tell," and remarked that this opera was one of her favourites.

It was not the hour for opera and my curiosity was piqued. Making enquiries afterwards, I found that the same air from "Guillaume Tell" was in fact being performed at a concert in the Champs Elysées at the very time when she told me that she heard it. Whether these actual tones reached her ears while her senses were in a state of hyperæsthesia, or whether she caught up the melody from the "Astral Light" I do not know, but I have since often been able to verify that she could at times hear what was taking place at a distance.

Nothing occurred during the evening at the Duchesse

de Pomar's that is worth recording, but when I left to go home to my hôtel Madame Blavatsky begged me to return to Enghien to see her the next day. This I did, and received a cordial invitation from the Comtesse d'Adhémar to take up my quarters with her, but of private conversation with H.P.B. there was no more than on the previous day. However, I had the pleasure of meeting Mr. William Q. Judge, who was acting as H.P.B.'s private secretary at that time, and many a pleasant talk we had in his hours of leisure, wandering about beneath the trees of the beautiful park.

Madame Blavatsky was shut up in her room all day, and I only met her at table and during the evenings, when she was surrounded by a *côterie*, and there was no opportunity for private talk. I have no doubt now that the difficulties I experienced in getting access to Madame Blavatsky, and the delays that occurred before she came to the point with me, were calculated, and were of the nature of a probation, but I had no suspicion of this at the time.

At last I became both anxious to return to Sweden and unwilling to encroach any longer on the hospitality of my hosts, so one day I took Mr. Judge aside and begged him to tell "the Old Lady" that, unless she had something of real importance to say to me, I should leave the next day. Shortly afterwards I was called to her room, and there followed a conversation which I shall never forget.

She told me many things that I thought were known only to myself, and ended by saying that, before two years had passed, I should devote my life wholly to Theosophy.

At the time I had reason to regard this as an utter impossibility, and, as any reticence on the subject might have been liable to misconstruction, I felt obliged to tel her so.

She only smiled, and replied: "Master says so, and therefore I know it to be true."

The following morning I took my leave of her, said farewell to the d'Adhémars, and departed. Mr. Judge accompanied me to the station and saw me off, and that night I was whirling along in the train, wondering whether her words would come true, and thinking how entirely unfitted I was for such a life, and how impossible it would be for me to break down all the barriers which rose before me, barring the way to the goal she had pointed out to my bewildered gaze.

CHAPTER III.

In the autumn of 1885 I was making preparations to leave my home in Sweden in order to spend the winter with some friends in Italy, and, incidentally, *en route* to pay Madame Gebhard a promised visit at her residence in Elberfeld.

It was while I was engaged in putting my affairs in order, in view of my long absence, that an incident occurred, not indeed singular in my experience, but out of the normal. I was arranging and laying aside the articles I intended to take with me to Italy, when I heard a voice saying:—" Take that book, it will be useful to you on your journey." I may as well say at once that I have the faculties of clairvoyance and clairaudience rather strongly developed. I turned my eyes on a manuscript volume I had placed among the heap of things to be locked away until my return. Certainly it seemed a singularly inappropriate *vade mecum* for a holiday, being a collection of notes on the " Tarot " and passages in the *Kabbalah* that had been compiled for me by a friend. However, I decided to take it with me, and laid the book in the bottom of one of my travelling trunks.

At last the day came for me to leave Sweden, in October, 1885, and I arrived at Elberfeld, where I met with a cordial and affectionate greeting from Madame Gebhard. The warmth of heart and steadfast friendship of this excellent woman were for years a source of comfort and support to me, as they were also to Madame Blavatsky, and my affection and admiration for her increased as I became better acquainted with the true and noble character which gradually unfolded itself before me.

It appeared that Madame Blavatsky and a party of Theosophists had spent some eight weeks with Madame Gebhard in the autumn of 1884, and she had many things to tell me of the interesting incidents that befel during that time. Thus I re-entered that sphere of influence which had made so deep an impression upon me at Enghien, and I felt all my interest in and enthusiasm for H. P. B. revive.

However, the time was drawing near for me to pass on into Italy. My friends never ceased pressing me to join them there, and at last the date of my departure was fixed.

When I told Madame Gebhard that I must leave her in a few days, she spoke to me of a letter she had received from H. P. B., in which she deplored her loneliness. She was ill in body and depressed in mind. Her sole companions were her servant and an Indian gentleman who had accompanied her from Bombay, and of whom I shall have to say a word later. "Go to her," said Madame Gebhard, "she needs sympathy, and you can cheer her. For me it is impossible, I have my duties, but you can befriend her if you will."

I thought the matter over. Certainly it was possible for me to comply with the request at the risk of disappointing my friends in Italy, but their plans would not be greatly disarranged, and I decided at length that if H.P.B desired my company I would go to her for a month before starting for the South. Thus, as she had predicted, and within the period she named, circumstances seemed to be drawing me back to her.

B

Madame Gebhard was genuinely pleased when I made known my decision to her and showed her a letter I had written to " the Old Lady " in Würzburg, suggesting that if she cared to receive me I would spend a few weeks with her, as Madame Gebhard had said she was in need of care and companionship. The letter was despatched, and we waited eagerly for the reply. When at last it lay upon the breakfast table there was much excitement in regard to its contents, but anticipation soon turned into consternation on Madame Gebhard's part and disappointment on mine, when we found nothing more nor less than a polite refusal beneath the seal—Madame Blavatsky was sorry, but she had no room for me; besides, she was so occupied in writing her *Secret Doctrine* that she had no time to entertain visitors, but hoped we might meet on my return from Italy. The tone was civil enough, and even amiable, but the intention seemed to be to convey to me unmistakably that I was not wanted.

Madame Gebhard's face fell as I read the letter aloud. To her, evidently, it was incomprehensible. As for me after the first natural disappointment at the frustration of plans arrived at not without difficulty, I set my face hopefully southward.

My luggage was soon ready, and a cab was actually waiting for me at the door when a telegram was put into my hands containing these words :—" Come to Würzburg at once, wanted immediately.—Blavatsky."

It may easily be imagined that this message took me by surprise, and in blank amazement I turned to Madame Gebhard for an explanation. But she was frankly delighted and radiant. Evidently all her thoughts, all her sympathies, were with her " Old Lady."

"Oh, she *does* want you, you see, after all," she cried. "Go to her, go." There was no resisting. I let my secret inclinations find excuse in the pressure of persuasion, and instead of taking my ticket to Rome I took one to Würzburg, and was soon travelling onwards to work out my Karma.

It was evening when I reached Madame Blavatsky's odgings, and as I mounted the stairs my pulse was a little hurried while I speculated upon the reception which awaited me. I knew nothing of the causes which had dictated this change at the very eleventh hour. The field of possibilities was wide enough to afford free scope for my imagination, which now pictured to me a serious and sudden illness as the cause of the telegram, and now amused me with the anticipation of a third change of mind that would land me in Rome after all within thirty-six hours. The event was equally removed from both these extremes.

Madame Blavatsky's welcome was a warm one, and, after the first few words of greeting, she remarked, "I have to apologise to you for behaving so strangely. I will tell you the truth, which is, that I did not want you. I have only one bedroom here, and I thought that you might be a fine lady and not care to share it with me. My ways are probably not your ways. If you came to me I knew that you would have to put up with many things that might seem to you intolerable discomforts. That is why I decided to decline your offer, and I wrote to you in that sense; but after my letter was posted Master spoke to me and said that I was to tell you to come. I never disobey a word from Master, and I telegraphed at once. Since then I have been trying to make the bedroom more habitable. I have bought a large screen which will divide the room, so that you can have one side and I the other, and I hope you will not be too uncomfortable."

I replied that whatever the surroundings to which I had been accustomed might have been, I would willingly relinquish them all for the pleasure of her companionship.

I remember very well that it was then, on going into the dining room together to take some tea, that she said to me abruptly, as of something that had been dwelling on her mind,

"Master says you have a book for me of which I am much in need."

"No, indeed," I replied, "I have no books with me."

"Think again," she said, "Master says you were told in Sweden to bring a book on the Tarot and the *Kabbalah*."

Then I recollected the circumstances that I have related above. From the time I had placed the volume in the bottom of my box it had been out of my sight and out of my mind. Now, when I hurried to the bedroom, unlocked the trunk, and dived to the bottom, I found it in the same corner I had left it when packing the box in Sweden, undisturbed from that moment to this. But this was not all. When I returned to the dining-room with it in my hand, Madame Blavatsky made a gesture and cried, "Stay, do not open it yet. Now turn to page ten and on the sixth line you will find the words . . ." And she quoted a passage.

I opened the book which, let it be remembered, was no printed volume of which there might be a copy in H.P.B.'s possession, but a manuscript album in which, as I have said, had been written notes and excerpts by a friend of mine for my own use, yet on the page and at the line she had indicated I found the very words she had uttered.

When I handed her the book I ventured to ask her why she wanted it.

"Oh," she replied, "for *The Secret Doctrine*. That is my new work that I am so busily engaged in writing. Master is collecting material for me. He knew you had the book and told you to bring it that it might be at hand for reference."

No work was done that first evening, but the next day I began to realise what the course of H. P. B.'s life was, and what mine was likely to be while I stayed with her.

CHAPTER IV.

THE description of a single day will serve to give an idea of the routine of her life at this time.

At six o'clock I was awakened by the servant coming with a cup of coffee for Madame Blavatsky, who, after this slight refreshment, rose and dressed, and by seven o'clock was at her desk in the sitting room.

She told me that this was her invariable habit, and that breakfast would be served at eight. After breakfast she settled herself at her writing desk and the day's work began in earnest. At one o'clock dinner was served, whereupon I rang a small hand-bell to call H. P. B. Sometimes she would come in at once, but at other times her door would remain closed hour after hour, until our Swiss maid would come to me, almost with tears in her eyes, to ask what was to be done about Madame's dinner, which was either getting cold or dried up, burnt, and utterly spoiled. At last H.P.B. would come in weary with so many hours of exhausting labour and fasting; then another dinner would be cooked, or I would send to the Hotel to get her some nourishing food.

At seven o'clock she laid aside her writing, and after tea we would spend a pleasant evening together.

Comfortably seated in her big armchair, H. P. B. used to arrange her cards for a game of Patience, as she said to rest her mind. It seems as if the mechanical process of laying her cards enabled her mind to free itself from the pressure of concentrated labour during the day's work. She never cared to talk of Theosophy in the evenings.

The mental tension during the day was so severe that she needed above all things rest, and so I procured as many journals and magazines as I could, and from these I would read the articles and passages that I thought most likely to interest and amuse her. At nine o'clock she went to bed, where she would surround herself with her Russian newspapers and read them until a late hour.

It was thus our days passed in the same routine; the only change worth noticing being that sometimes she would leave the door open between her writing room and the dining room where I sat, and then from time to time we would converse together, or I would write letters for her, or discuss the contents of those we had received.

Our visitors were very few. Once a week the doctor called to enquire after H. P. B.'s health, and he would stay gossiping for more than an hour. Sometimes but rarely, our landlord, a Jew of material tendencies, would tell a good story of life as he saw it through his spectacles, and many a laugh we all had together —a pleasant interruption to the daily monotony of our work.

At this time I learned little more concerning *The Secret Doctrine* than that it was to be a work far more voluminous than *Isis Unveiled*, that it would consist when complete of four volumes, and that it would give out to the world as much of the esoteric doctrine as was possible at the present stage of human evolution. "It will, of course, be very fragmentary," she said, "and there will of necessity be great gaps left, but it will make men think, and as soon as they are ready more will be given out. But," she added after a pause, "that will not be until the next century, when men will begin to understand and discuss this book intelligently."

Soon, however, I was entrusted with the task of making fair copies of H.P.B.'s manuscript, and then of course I began to get glimpses of the subject matter of *The Secret Doctrine*.

I have previously not alluded to the presence at Würzburg of a Hindu gentleman, who, for a time, was a prominent figure in our little society.

It was at Adyar one day that an Indian, begrimed with dirt, clad in tattered garments, and with a miserable expression of countenance, made his way into Madame Blavatsky's presence. He cast himself at her feet and with tears in his voice and eyes entreated her to save him. On enquiry it appeared that in a mood of religious exaltation he had wandered away into the jungle with the intention of renouncing society, becoming a "forest-dweller," and devoting himself to religious contemplation and yoga practices. Here he had joined a yogi who was willing to accept him as his chela or pupil, and had spent some time in study of the difficult and dangerous system of "Hatha Yog," a system which relies almost exclusively on physiological processes for the development of psychic powers.

At last, overcome by terror at his experiences, and the formidable training he had to undergo, he made his escape from his Guru. By what circumstances he was led to H. P. B. does not appear, but he reached her, and she comforted him and calmed his mind, clothed and fed him, and then, at his request, began to teach him the truly spiritual path of development, the Raja Yoga philosophy. In return he vowed a life-long devotion, and when she left India for Europe he persuaded her to bring him with her.

He was a little man, of nervous temperament, with bright beady eyes. During the first few days that I spent at Würzburg he was for ever talking to me, translating stories from his Tamil books, and relating all sorts of wonderful adventures that had happened to him when he was in the forest with his Hatha Yog master. But he did not remain long in Würzburg. Madame Gebhard sent him a cordial invitation to pay her a visit at Elberfeld, and so one morning, after an effusive scene of leave-taking with H.P.B., during which he declared she had been more than a mother to him, that the days he had spent with her had been the happiest of his life, he departed—I regret to say never to return. Too soon flattery turned his head and his heart, and the poor little man was false to all that should have been most sacred to him.

I wish to pass very lightly over incidents such as this, which, I am sorry to say, was not an isolated instance of ingratitude and desertion, but was, perhaps, the one which affected H.P.B. most painfully. I mention it here to show an example of the mental distress which, added to physical maladies and weakness, rendered progress with her task slow and painful.

The quiet studious life that I have tried to describe continued for some little time, and the work progressed steadily, until, one morning, a thunderbolt descended upon us. By the early post, without a word of warning, H.P.B. received a copy of the well-known *Report of the Society for Psychical Research*. It was a cruel blow, and, in the form it took, wholly unexpected. I shall never forget that day nor the look of blank and stony despair that she cast on me when I entered her sitting-room and found her with the book open in her hands.

"This," she cried, "is the Karma of the Theosophical Society, and it falls upon me. I am the scapegoat. I am made to bear all the sins of the Society, and now that I am dubbed the greatest impostor of the age, and a Russian spy into the bargain, who will listen to me or read *The Secret Doctrine* ? How can I carry on Master's work ? O cursed phenomena, which I only produced to please private friends and instruct those around me. What an awful Karma to bear! How shall I live through it ? If I die Master's work will be wasted, and the Society will be ruined!"

In the intensity of her passion at first she would not listen to reason, but turned against me, saying, "Why don't you go ? Why don't you leave me ? You are a Countess, you cannot stop here with a ruined woman, with one held up to scorn before the whole world, one who will be pointed at everywhere as a trickster and an impostor. Go before you are defiled by my shame."

"H.P.B.," I said, as my eyes met hers with a steady gaze, "you know that Master lives and that He is your Master, and that the Theosophical Society was founded by Him. How, then, can it perish ? And since I know this as well as you, since for me, now, the truth has been placed beyond the possibility of doubt, how can you for one moment suppose that I could desert you and the Cause we both are pledged to serve ? Why, if every member of the Theosophical Society should prove traitor to that Cause you and I would remain, and would wait and work until the good times come again."

Letters came in containing nothing but recrimination and abuse, resignation of Fellows, and apathy and fear on the part of those who remained. It was a trying time;

the very existence of the Theosophical Society seemed threatened, and H.P.B. felt as if it were crumbling away from under her feet.

Her sensitive nature was too deeply wounded, her indignation and resentment at unmerited wrong too strongly stirred, to listen at first to counsels of patience and moderation. Nothing would serve but she must start for London at once and annihilate her enemies in the flames of her just wrath. At last, however, I pacified her, but only for a time. Every post only increased her anger and despair, and for a long time no useful work could be done. She recognised at last that for her there was no hope or remedy in legal proceedings in this country any more than in India. This is proved by a passage from a "Protest" which she contributed to Mr. Sinnett's reply to the *Report* entitled "'Occult World Phenomena' and the Society for Psychical Research," and which I will quote.

"Mr. Hodgson knows," she wrote, "and the Committee doubtless share his knowledge, that he is safe from actions for libel at my hands, because I have no money to conduct costly proceedings (having given all I ever had to the cause I serve), and also because my vindication would involve the examination into psychic mysteries which cannot be dealt fairly with in a court of law; and again, because there are questions which I am solemnly pledged never to answer, but which a legal investigation of these slanders would inevitably bring to the front, while my silence and refusal to answer certain queries would be misconstrued into 'contempt of court.' This condition of things explains the shameless attack that has been made upon an almost defenceless woman, and the inaction in face of it to which I am so cruelly condemned."

I may quote, too, to supplement my own account of this

trying time, Mr. Sinnett's impressions in regard to it given in "*Incidents in the Life of Madame Blavatsky.*"

"For a whole fortnight," he says, "the tumult of Madame Blavatsky's emotions rendered any further progress with her work impossible. Her volcanic temperament renders her in all emergencies a very bad exponent of her own case, whatever that may be. The letters, memoranda and protests on which she wasted her energies during this miserable fortnight were few, if any, of a kind that would have helped a cold and unsympathetic public to understand the truth of things, and it is not worth while to resuscitate them here. I induced her to tone down one protest into a presentable shape for insertion in a pamphlet I issued in the latter part of January, and for the rest few but her most intimate friends would correctly appreciate their fire and fury. Her language, when she is in fits of excitement, would lead a stranger to suppose her thirsting for revenge, beside herself with passion, ready to exact savage vengeance on her enemies if she had the power. It is only those who know her as intimately as half-a-dozen of her closest friends may, who are quite aware through all this effervescence of feeling that if her enemies were really put suddenly in her power, her rage against them would collapse like a broken soap-bubble."

To conclude this episode I may perhaps be permitted to quote a letter of my own, addressed to Mr. Sinnett at that time and published in his book* and in the American newspaper press, where I summarize some impressions of my stay at Würzburg. I shall omit the first paragraph, which deals only with what I have already described.

' . . . . HAVING heard the absurd rumours circulating against her (H. P. B.) and by which she was accused of practising black magic, fraud and deception, I was on my guard, and went to her in a calm and tranquil frame of mind, determined to

* *Incidents in the Life of Madame Blavatsky.*

accept nothing of an occult character coming from her without sufficient proof; to make myself positive, to keep my eyes open, and to be just and true in my conclusions. Common sense would not permit me to believe in her guilt without proof, but if that proof had been furnished, my sense of honour would have made it impossible for me to remain in a Society, the founder of which committed cheating and trickery: therefore my frame of mind was bent on investigation, and I was anxious to find out the *truth*.

"I have now spent a few months with Madame Blavatsky. I have shared her room and been with her morning, noon and night. I have had access to all her boxes and drawers, have read the letters which she received and those which she wrote, and I now openly and honestly declare that I am ashamed of myself for having ever suspected her, for I believe her to be an honest and true woman, faithful to death to her Masters, and to the cause for which she has sacrificed position, fortune and health. There is no doubt in my mind that she made these sacrifices, for I have seen the proofs of them, some of which consisted of documents whose genuineness is above all suspicion.

"From a worldly point of view Madame Blavatsky is an unhappy woman, slandered, doubted, and abused by many; but, looked at from a higher point of view, she has extraordinary gifts, and no amount of vilification can deprive her of the privileges which she enjoys, and which consist in a know edge of many things that are known to only a few mortals, and in a personal intercourse with certain Eastern Adepts.

"On account of the extensive knowledge which she ossesses, and which extends far into the invisible part of nature, is very much to be regretted that all her troubles and trials pr event her giving to the world a great deal of information, which she would be willing to impart if she were permitted to remain undisturbed and in peace.

"Even the great work in which she is now engaged, *The Secret Doctrine*, has been greatly impeded by all the persecutions, offensive letters, and other petty annoyances, to which she has been subjected this winter; for it should be remembered that H. P. Blavatsky is not herself a full-grown Adept, nor does she claim to be one, and that, therefore, in spite of all her knowledge, she is as painfully sensitive to insult and suspicion as any lady of refinement in her position could be expected to be.

"*The Secret Doctrine* will be indeed a great and grand work. I have had the privilege of watching its progress, of reading the manuscripts, and of witnessing the occult way in which she derived her information.

"I have latterly heard, among people who style themselves 'Theosophists,' expressions which surprised and pained me. Some such persons said that 'if it were proven that the Mahatmas did not exist, it would not matter, that Theosophy was nevertheless a truth, &c., &c.' Such and similar statements have come into circulation in Germany, England and America; but to my understanding they are very erroneous, for, in the first place, if there were no Mahatmas or Adepts—that is to say, persons who have progressed so far in the scale of human evolution as to be able to unite their personality with the sixth principle of the universe (the universal Christ)—then the teachings of that system which has been called 'Theosophy' would be false; because there would be a break in the scale of progression, which would be more difficult to account for than the absence of the 'missing link' of Darwin. But if these persons refer merely to those Adepts who are said to have been active in the foundation of the 'Theosophical Society,' they seem to forget that without these Adepts we would never have had that society, nor would *Isis Unveiled*, *Esoteric Buddhism*, *Light on the Path*, *The Theosophist*, and other valuable Theosophical publications have ever been written; and if, in the future, we should shut ourselves out from the influence of the Mahatmas, and be left entirely to our own resources, we should soon become lost in a labyrinth of metaphysical speculation. It must be left to science and speculative philosophy to confine themselves to theories, and to the obtaining of such information as is contained in books: Theosophy goes farther, and acquires knowledge by direct interior perception.

The study of Theosophy means therefore *practical development*, and to attain this development a guide is necessary who knows that which he teaches, and who must have attained himself that state by the process of *spiritual regeneration*.

"After all that has been said in Mr. Sinnett's *Memoirs* about the Occult phenomena taking place in the presence of Madame Blavatsky, and how such phenomena have been a part and parcel of her life, occurring at all times, both with and without her knowledge, I need only add that during my stay with her I have frequently witnessed such genuine phenomena. Here, as in every other department in life, the main point is to learn to discriminate properly, and to estimate everything at its true value.

"Yours sincerely,
"CONSTANCE WACHTMEISTER, F.T.S."

CHAPTER V.

IT is little to be wondered at that the progress of *The Secret Doctrine* was brought to a standstill during these stormy days, and that when, at last, the work was resumed, the necessary detachment and tranquillity of mind were found hard of attainment.

H.P.B. said to me one evening: "You cannot imagine what it is to feel so many adverse thoughts and currents directed against you; it is like the prickings of a thousand needles, and I have continually to be erecting a wall of protection around me." I asked her whether she knew from whom these unfriendly thoughts came, she answered: "Yes; unfortunately I do, and I am always trying to shut my eyes so as not to see and know"; and to prove to me that this was the case, she would tell me of letters that had been written, quoting passages from them, and these actually arrived a day or two afterwards, I being able to verify the correctness of the sentences.

One day at this time, when I walked into H.P.B.'s writing room, I found the floor strewn with sheets of discarded manuscript. I asked the meaning of this scene of confusion, and she replied: "Yes, I have tried twelve times to write this one page correctly, and each time Master says it is wrong. I think I shall go mad, writing it so often; but leave me alone; I will not pause until I have conquered it, even if I have to go on all night."

I brought a cup of coffee to refresh and sustain her, and then left her to prosecute her weary task. An hour later

I heard her voice calling me, and on entering found that, at last, the passage was completed to satisfaction, but the labour had been terrible, and the results were often at this time small and uncertain.

As she leant back enjoying her cigarette and the sense of relief from arduous effort, I rested on the arm of her great chair and asked her how it was she could make mistakes in setting down what was given to her. She said: " Well, you see, what I do is this. I make what I can only describe as a sort of vacuum in the air before me, and fix my sight and my will upon it, and soon scene after scene passes before me like the successive pictures of a diorama, or, if I need a reference or information from some book, I fix my mind intently, and the astral counterpart of the book appears, and from it I take what I need. The more perfectly my mind is freed from distractions and mortifications, the more energy and intentness it possesses, the more easily I can do this; but to-day, after all the vexations I have undergone in consequence of the letter from X., I could not concentrate properly, and each time I tried I got the quotations all wrong. Master says it is right now, so let us go in and have some tea."

I have already remarked how few were our visitors at this time. This evening, however, I was surprised to hear the sound of a strange voice in the passage, and soon afterwards a German professor, whose name I need not give, was announced.

He excused his intrusion ; he had travelled many miles, he said, to see Madame Blavatsky, and to express his sympathy. He was aware of the animus and unfairness that characterised the S.P.R. *Report* and now, would not Madame favour him with an exhibition, in the interests of psychic science, of some of the "phenomena" she could so easily produce?

Now "the Old Lady" was very tired, and perhaps she had not too much faith in the suave professions of her visitor; anyhow, she was very disinclined to gratify him, but at last, overpersuaded by his entreaties, she consented to produce some trifling experiments in psycho-electric force—raps—the simplest, easiest, and most familiar of these "phenomena."

She begged him to draw away the table that stood in front of her to some distance, so that he could pass freely round it and inspect it on all sides. "Now," she said, "I will rap for you on that table as many times as you please." He asked first for three times, then five times, then seven times, and so on, and as H.P.B. raised her finger, pointing it at the table, there came sharp, distinct raps in accordance with his expressed wish.

The Professor seemed delighted. He skipped round the table with wonderful agility, he peeped under it, he examined it on all sides, and when H.P.B. was too exhausted to gratify his curiosity in this direction any longer, he sat down and plied her with questions, to all of which she replied with her usual vivacity and charm of manner.

At length our visitor took his departure—unconvinced, as we afterwards learned. He was a disciple of Huxley, and preferred to adopt any explanation, however absurd, provided it did not clash with his own theories.

Poor H.P.B.! Her swollen and painful limbs, that could hardly bear her from chair to couch, were little fitted for the gymnastics the Professor credited them with.

The circumstance which, perhaps, more than any other

attracted my attention and excited my wonder when I began to help Madame Blavatsky as her amanuensis, and thus got some glimpses of the nature of her work upon *The Secret Doctrine*, was the poverty of her travelling library. Her manuscripts were full to overflowing with references, quotations, allusions, from a mass of rare and recondite works on subjects of the most varied kind. Now she needed verification of a passage from some book only to be found at the Vatican, and again from some document of which only the British Museum possessed a copy. Yet it was only verification she needed. The matter she had, however she may have gained it—certainly she could not have procured her information from the handful of very ordinary books she carried about with her.

Shortly after my arrival in Würzburg she took occasion to ask me if I knew anyone who could go for her to the Bodleian Library. It happened that I did know someone I could ask, so my friend verified a passage that H.P.B. had seen in the Astral Light, with the title of the book, the chapter, page and figures all correctly noted.

Such visions often present the image of the original reversed, as it might be seen in a looking-glass, and though words can, with a little practice, be read easily, and the general sense and context prevent serious error, it is much more difficult to avoid mistakes in figures, and it was figures that were in question on this occasion.

Once a very difficult task was assigned to me, namely, to verify a passage taken from a manuscript in the Vatican. Having made the acquaintance of a gentleman who had a relative in the Vatican, I with some difficulty succeeded in verifying the passage. Two words were wrong, but all the remainder correct, and, strangely enough, I was told that these words, being considerably blurred, were difficult to decipher.

These are but a few instances out of many. If ever H.P.B. wanted definite information on any subject which came uppermost in her writing, that information was sure to reach her in one way or another, either in a communication from a friend at a distance, in a newspaper or a magazine, or in the course of our casual reading of books; and this happened with a frequency and appositeness that took it quite out of the region of mere coincidence. She would, however, use normal means in preference to the abnormal when possible, so as not to exhaust her power unnecessarily.

I was not alone in remarking the assistance that came unsought to H.P.B. in the prosecution of her task, and the accuracy of the quotations that she received, and I insert here a note sent me by Miss E. Kislingbury, which illustrates the point and sets it in a strong light.

"After the publication of the now famous Psychical Society's Report, of which I felt strongly the injustice, I determined to go and see Madame Blavatsky, then living, I was told, at Würzburg. I found her living quietly in the quaint old German town, with the Countess Wachtmeister, who had stayed with her all the winter. She was ill, suffering from a complication of disorders, and under constant medical treatment. She was harassed, mentally, by the defection of friends and the petty assaults of enemies, in consequence of the above named Report, and yet, in face of all these difficulties, H.P.B. was engaged on the colossal task of writing *The Secret Doctrine*. In a foreign town, the language of whose inhabitants was unfamiliar to her, with only such books as she had carried with her from India, far from any friends who could have helped her in finding needful references or making useful notes, she toiled away, rarely leaving her desk, except for meals, from early morning till six o'clock in the evening. But H.P.B. had her invisible helpers as she sat writing in the room sacred to her work. As I was not at that time a member of the T.S., though I had known H.P.B. almost since its foundation, little was said either *to* me or *before* me of the methods used. One day, however, she brought me a paper with a quotation which had been given her from some Catholic writer on the relation between science and religion, and asked whether I could help her in verifying it, as to the author and work in which it occurred. It struck me, from the nature of the quotation, that it might be from Cardinal Wiseman's *Lectures on Science and Religion*, and I wrote to a friend in London, with the result that the verification was complete, chapter and page being found, as it now stands in *The Secret Doctrine*, vol. II., p. 704."

CHAPTER VI.

ANOTHER incident of frequent occurrence came under my notice from time to time, and marks another mode in which guidance and aid were given to H.P.B. in her work. Often, in the early morning, I would see on her writing-table a piece of paper with unfamiliar characters traced upon it in red ink. On asking her what was the meaning of these mysterious notes, she replied that they indicated her work for the day.

These were examples of the "precipitated" messages which have been the subject of so much heated controversy, even within the ranks of the Theosophical Society, and of endless unintelligent ridicule without—"the 'red and blue spook-like messages,' as X. truly calls them," to quote from a letter of H.P.B., written about this time, and since published in *The Path*. In the same letter she goes on to say :—

"Was it *fraud?* *Certainly not*. Was it written and produced by elementals? NEVER. It was delivered, and the *physical* phenomena are produced by elementals used for the purpose, but what have they, those senseless beings, to do with the intelligent portions of the smallest and most foolish message?"

It is, perhaps, little to be wondered at that such messages should, in the present state of ignorance in regard to the possibilities of psychic phenomena, be received with suspicion. The best that could be hoped from the average man or woman would be a suspension of judgment, accompanied by a willingness to learn and investigate. But when we come to examine H.P.B.'s own behaviour in presence of these messages we get an incontrovertible proof of her *bonâ fides*. To her they came direct, and the injunctions they contained were always met by her with submission and obedience, even when she would have preferred to act otherwise.

How often, then, did I grieve over reams of manuscript, carefully prepared and copied, and, at a word, an intimation from the Masters, consigned to the flames—stores of information and commentary that it seems to me would be of priceless value to us now that we have lost our Teacher.

At that time, it is true, I understood very little of what I copied, and did not realise the value of the teachings as I do now. I have often since thought that I was the more fitted for my task on that very account, since, as only fragments and hints are given out in *The Secret Doctrine*, H.P.B. may in the early days have set down much that it was not advisable to make known to anyone, even to one who, like myself, was an earnest though untried pupil. Indeed, I know for a fact that much really esoteric teaching had to be weeded out of her original writings, and, as I have said, much both of her MSS. and my copies was destroyed. At that time, too, I never got any satisfactory answers to my enquiries, so that at last I learned to be silent and rarely or never asked a question.

It is very difficult for those who enter the Theosophical Society now to realise the condition of things at the time of which I am writing. At that time no such opportunities for study and progress were afforded to the student of Theosophy as are now lavished upon the candidate for membership, and the applicant for instruction. Then there were no lectures and very few books. H.P.B. herself was constitutionally, and by the innate turn of her mind, unfitted for the task of orderly and patient exposition of her teachings. I have before me a letter of hers, undated, but written about this time from Elberfeld, whither she went after Würzburg, which gives a vivid picture of her droll despair at having such a burden imposed upon her. I give the extracts from her correspondence verbatim, for the quaintness of her phraseology was a peculiar characteristic of her own, and it is well known that as yet her English was very imperfect.

"If you are 'distressed'," she writes to me, "I am at an utter loss to understand what is *expected* of me! I have never promised to play guru, schoolmaster, or professor for Y., or any one else. Master told *him* to go to Elberfeld, and Master told *me* that he was to come and that I would have to answer his questions. I have done so, and can do no more. I have read to him from the *S.D.* and found I could not proceed, for he interrupted me at every line, and not only with questions, but generally made a dissertation as an answer to his own question, which answer lasted twenty minutes. As for Y., he will answer you for himself, as I made him write to you. I told you repeatedly that I have *never* taught anyone but in my own usual way. Olcott and Judge have learnt all they know by associating with me. If I had to be inflicted the punishment of giving regular instructions in a professor-like way for *one* hour, let alone two in a day, I would rather run away to the North Pole or die any day, severing my connection with Theosophy entirely. I am incapable of it, as everyone *ought to know* who knows me. To this day I could not make out what Y. wants to know. Is it Occultism, Metaphysics, or the principles of Theosophy in general? If the former, I find him absolutely unfit for it! We have made a pledge (that M. G. will send you) and Y. insisted on including among the members of that secret pledge his wife, and now, when we have signed it, we find that he has no idea of using his will-power, and that his wife thinks it SINFUL (!!) So what's the use? As to Metaphysics, he can learn them from M. I told him that M. knows nothing of our Occult doctrines, and could not teach him, but he can explain to him *Bhagavad Gitâ* better than I can. . . . That's all I can say. I am sick and nervous more than ever. The current of the *S.D.* has stopped, and it will take two months before I can regain that state in which I was at Würzburg. To write it I must be left entirely quiet, and if I am to be bothered with *teachings*, then I must give up the *S.D.* Let people choose and see which is more useful—that the *S.D.* should be written or Y. instructed."

A privileged individual in these early days might perhaps get into correspondence with an older member, but, at best, the difficulties were great, and it was only a determined will to overcome all obstacles, and, one may perhaps add, a Karmic inheritance of natural aptitude, that could supply by inherent energy the lack of the facilities that are now so generously presented.

Then, in our most sanguine moments, we never dreamed of a large society with American, Indian and European Sections, and with numerous branches and centres of activity in almost every important country of the world. It seemed to us that all that could be hoped for was a scanty band of faithful students, a group of earnest disciples, to keep alight the sparks of occult teachings until the last quarter of the twentieth century, when, with the advent of a new minor cycle, a fresh access of spiritual light might be looked for.

But as even these few years have slipped by, and though they have robbed us of the bodily presence of our Teacher, we have come to learn a different lesson; we have been forced to recognise how we miscalculated the strength of the spiritual forces behind the movement. It becomes clearer and clearer, day by day, that Theosophy, in its broad outlines at least, is no exclusive privilege of a favoured few, but is a free gift to humanity at large, and that in its influence on the current of modern thought it must survive as a potent factor against the pessimistic materialism of the age.

CHAPTER VII.

Living in such close and familiar intercourse with H.P.B. as I did at this time, it naturally happened that I was a witness of many of the "phenomena" which took place in her vicinity.

There was one occurrence, continuously repeated over a long period, which impressed me very strongly with the conviction that she was watched and cared for by unseen guardians. From the first night that I passed in her room, until the last that preceded our departure from Würzburg, I heard a regularly intermittent series of raps on the table by her bedside. They would begin at ten o'clock each evening, and would continue, at intervals of ten minutes, until six o'clock in the morning. They were sharp, clear raps, such as I never heard at any other time. Sometimes I held my watch in my hand for an hour at a stretch, and always as the ten minute interval ticked itself out, the rap would come with the utmost regularity. Whether H.P.B. was awake or asleep mattered nothing to the occurrence of the phenomenon, nor to its uniformity.

When I asked for an explanation of these raps I was told that it was an effect of what might be called a sort of psychic telegraph, which placed her in communication with her Teachers, and that the chelas might watch her body while her astral left it.

In this connection I may mention another incident that proved to me that there were agencies at work in her neighbourhood whose nature and action were inexplicable on generally accepted theories of the constitution and laws of matter.

As I have already remarked, H.P.B. was accustomed to read her Russian newspapers at night after retiring, and it was rarely that she extinguished her lamp before midnight. There was a screen between my bed and this lamp, but, nevertheless, its powerful rays, reflected from ceiling and walls, often disturbed my rest. One night this lamp was burning after the clock had struck one. I could not sleep, and, as I heard by H.P.B.'s regular breathing that she slept, I rose, gently walked round to the lamp, and turned it out. There was always a dim light pervading the bedroom, which came from a night-light burning in the study, the door between that room and the bedroom being kept open. I had extinguished the lamp, and was going back, when it flamed up again, and the room was brightly illuminated. I thought to myself—what a strange lamp, I suppose the spring does not act, so I put my hand again on the spring, and watched until every vestige of flame was extinct, and, even then, held down the spring for a minute. Then I released it and stood for a moment longer watching, when, to my surprise, the flame reappeared and the lamp was burning as brightly as ever. This puzzled me considerably, and I determined to stand there by that lamp and put it out all through the night, if necessary, until I discovered the why and wherefore of its eccentricities. For the third time I pressed the spring and turned it down until the lamp was quite out, and then released it, watching eagerly to see what would take place. For the third time the lamp burned up, and this time I saw a brown hand slowly and gently turning the knob of the lamp. Familiar as I was with the action of astral forces and astral entities on the physical plane, I had no difficulty in coming to the conclusion that it was the hand of a chelâ, and, surmising that there was some reason why the lamp should remain alight, I returned to my couch. But a spirit of perversity and curiosity dwelt within me that night. I wanted to know more, so I called out, "Madame Blavatsky!" then, louder, "Madame Blavatsky!" and again "Madame Blavatsky!" Suddenly I heard an answering cry—"Oh, my heart! my heart! Countess, you have nearly killed me;" and then again, "My heart! my heart!" I flew to H.P.B.'s bedside. "I was with Master," she murmured, "why did you call me back?" I was thoroughly alarmed, for her heart fluttered under my hand with wild palpitation.

I gave her a dose of digitalis, and sat beside her until the symptoms had abated and she had become calmer. Then she told me how Col. Olcott had once nearly killed her in the same way, by calling her back suddenly when her astral form was absent from her body. She made me promise that I would never try experiments with her again, and this promise I readily gave, out of the fulness of my grief and contrition for having caused her such suffering.

But why, it will be asked, did she continue to suffer, with powers at her command which could relieve suffering? Why, when she was labouring at so important a task through long hours of every day—a task that needed a mind untroubled and a sound body—why did she never stretch out a finger to amend the conditions and to banish weakness and pain that would have prostrated any ordinary person completely?

The question is a natural one, and it did not fail to occur to me, knowing as I did the healing powers she possessed, and her capacity to alleviate the pains of others.

When the question was put to her, her answer was invariably the same.

"In occultism," she said, "a most solemn vow has to be taken never to use any powers acquired or conferred for the benefit of one's own personal self, for to do so would be to set foot on the steep and treacherous slope that ends in the abyss of Black Magic. I have taken that vow, and I am not one to break a pledge the sanctity of which cannot be brought within the comprehension of the profane. I would rather suffer any tortures than be untrue to my pledge. As for securing more favourable conditions for the execution of my task:—it is not with us that the end is held to justify the means, nor is it we who are permitted to do evil that good may come. And," she went on, "it is not only bodily pain and weakness, and the ravages of disease that I am to suffer with what patience I may, subduing them by my will for the sake of the work, but mental pain, ignominy, opprobrium and ridicule."

All this was no exaggeration, no mere form of emotional expression. It was true and remained true until her death, both in fact and in the history of the society. Upon her, standing in the forefront of the ranks of the Theosophical Society, fell the poisoned darts of reprobation and misrepresentation, as upon a living sensitive shield or bulwark, behind which the real culprits, the weak and erring ones, were concealed and protected.

She was, as it were, a sacrificial victim accepting a long martyrdom, and upon her agony, and the shame which she bore so undeservedly and bravely, was built up the prosperity of the Theosophical Society.

Very few members of the Theosophical Society are in a position to realise this. It is only those who have lived with her day by day, who have seen her hourly sufferings, and the tortures she endured from slanders and insults, and have, at the same time, watched the growth and prosperity of the Society in the comparatively calm and genial atmosphere secured to it by the shelter her conspicuous personality afforded, who can judge of the greatness of the debt they owe her, while too many do not even suspect their indebtedness.

CHAPTER VIII.

ONE day a temptation came to her in the form of a large yearly salary if she would write for the Russian papers. She might write, she was told, on occultism or any other subject which pleased her, if she would only contribute to their columns. Here was a promise of comfort and ease for the remainder of her life. Two hours' labour every day would be ample to satisfy all demands made on her time; but then no *Secret Doctrine* would be written. I spoke of a compromise, and asked her if it would not be possible for her to accept this engagement, and, at the same time, continue her Theosophical work. "No—a thousand times no!" she answered. "To write such a work as *The Secret Doctrine* I must have all my thoughts turned in the direction of that current. It is difficult enough even now, hampered as I am with this sick and worn-out old body, to get all I want, how much more difficult, then, if I am to be continually changing the currents into other directions. I have no longer the vitality or the energy left in me. Too much of it was exhausted at the time when I produced my phenomena."

"Why, then, did you make these phenomena?" I asked her.

"Because people were continually bothering me," she replied. "It was always, 'Oh, do materialise this,' or, 'do let me hear the astral bells,' and so on, and then I did not like to disappoint them. I acceded to their request. Now I have to suffer for it!" So the letter was written to Russia containing the refusal of the splendid offer, and one more sacrifice was made in order that the Theosophical Society might live and prosper. Many people have remarked to me, at different times, how foolish it was that "phenomena" should ever have been connected with the Theosophical Society or that H. P. B. should ever have wasted her time over such trivialities. To these remarks H. P. B. has invariably given the same answer, namely, that at the time when the Theosophical Society was formed it was necessary to draw the attention of the public to the fact, and that phenomena served this object more effectually than anything else could have done. Had H. P. B. given herself out in the first instance as simply a teacher of philosophy, very few students would have been drawn to her side, for, twenty years ago, many people had not reached the point at which they have now arrived. Freedom of thought and opinion were of rarer occurrence, and the study and the thought which are necessary for a true appreciation of Theosophy would have frightened them away. Education was at a lower level then than it is at the present day, and it required an attraction, such as is provided by the love of the marvellous, to awaken in them that initial interest which was destined to make them think more deeply. And so phenomena started the Society, but, having once introduced this element, it was difficult to get rid of it when it had served its turn. All came eager to have their sense of wonder gratified, and, when disappointed, went away wrathful and indignant.

We had a small, but very comfortable, apartment in Würzburg; the rooms were of a good size, lofty, and on the ground floor, so as to enable H. P. B. to go out and in with comfort. But during all the time that I was with her I could only persuade her to take fresh air three times. She seemed to enjoy these drives, but the trouble and exertion of preparing for them wearied her, and she esteemed them mere loss of time. I was in the habit, if possible, of going out daily for half an hour, as I felt that both air and exercise were necessary for my health, and I recall a curious incident which happened to me in connection with one of these walks. I was walking in one of the most frequented parts of the town, and, as I passed a perfumer's shop, I saw some soap in a glass bowl in the window. Remembering that I required some, I walked into the shop and chose a piece from the bowl. I saw the shopman wrap paper around it, took the parcel from his hand, put it in my pocket, and continued my walk. When I returned to my apartment I went straight to my room, without first going to see H.P.B., and took off my hat and cloak. Taking the parcel out of my pocket, I began to unfasten the string and pull off the wrappings, and, as I did so, I perceived a small sheet of folded paper inside. I could not help thinking, how fond people are of advertisements, they even stick them on a cake of soap! but then I suddenly remembered that I had seen the man fasten up the parcel, and that he assuredly had not inserted any. This struck me as strange, and, as the paper had fallen to the ground, I stooped down and picked it up, opened it, and there found a few remarks addressed to me from H.P.B.'s Master in His handwriting, which I had often seen before. They were an explanation of events which had been puzzling me for some days past, and gave me some directions as to my future course of action. This phenomenon was peculiarly interesting to me as having taken place without H.P.B.'s knowledge, and independently of her, for she was writing quite unconcernedly at her table in her writing room at the time, as I ascertained later on.

Since H.P.B.'s death, letters have been received from this same Master by various persons, showing his action as independent from that of H.P.B., but it was interesting to witnes this even during her lifetime, and I recall another incident where a phenomenon of a similar nature occurred. Dr. Hartmann had written me a letter requesting me to ascertain something from the Master relative to himself. I showed the letter to H.P.B. and asked her if she would communicate. She replied, "No, see what you can do with it yourself. Put it on Master's portrait, and if Master wishes to reply to Hartmann, the letter will be taken." I closed H.P.B.'s door and went to my writing table, where a portrait in oils of the Master was standing, placed the letter in the frame, took up a book, and read for about half an hour, nobody coming into the room during that time. When I looked up the letter was gone. A few days passed, during which I heard nothing. But one evening, on receiving the letters from the postman, I saw one from Dr. Hartmann, and thought to myself how bulky it was, and how strange that more postage should not have been charged on it. When I opened the envelope I took out first the Doctor's letter which I had placed on the portrait, then a letter from the Master answering Hartmann's questions, and lastly, the fresh letter from the Doctor, on the margin of which were annotations made in Master's handwriting relative to the matter contained in the letter. On the outside of Hartmann's letter was a seal with Master's signature precipitated on the envelope.

Phenomena such as these were constantly occurring. Letters received were frequently annotated inside in Master's handwriting, comments being made on what was written, or else letters disappeared for several days and, when returned, remarks were made as to contents. The first time this happened to me it caused me a good deal of surprise. Early one morning, at the breakfast table (letters were mostly brought to us by the first post), H.P.B. received several letters which she was immediately occupied in reading. I found one from Sweden which caused me some perplexity. Not knowing how to answer it, I placed it on the table beside me and went on eating my breakfast, cogitating over the contents. I soon finished my repast and, getting up, put out my hand to take the letter. It was gone. I searched under my plate, on the ground, in my pocket, but could find it nowhere. H.P.B. glanced up from the Russian letter she was reading and said, "What are you looking for?" I replied, "For a letter I received this morning." She said quietly, "It is useless to look for it. Master was by your side just now and I saw him take up an envelope." Three days passed without any news of this letter, when one morning as I was busy writing in the dining room, I suddenly saw the envelope on the blotting pad before me, and on the margin of the letter were comments with intimations as to how I should act, and later experience proved to me how wise the advice was. This I have invariably found to be the case, and had I always acted in accordance with advice given me from this source I should have been saved both monetary loss and a good deal of worry and trouble. It was in this wise. I had purchased in Sweden, some years previously, a small estate near the seaside. It was a lovely place. Both time and thought were spent in repairing and furnishing the house, in arranging the gardens and park, in which I took great pride. One day H.P.B. said to me, "I wonder you do not sell your estate in Sweden, because then you would be more free to work for Theosophy." I replied, "Oh! H.P.B., how can you ask me to do that? I should not like to part with my home after all the trouble and expense it has caused me, and besides I feel sure my son would be opposed to my selling it. I should also probably have much difficulty in finding a purchaser." To which H.P.B. replied, "Master wished me to tell you that if you will at once offer your estate for sale you will be able to dispose of it without loss. Master has told you this because he knows you want to work for Theosophy, and it will be the saving of much trouble to you if you do so at once." But I would not listen to her. In my inner heart I thought: H.P.B. wants me to sell the estate so as to bind me more closely to Theosophy. My friends are writing to me on all sides, saying that she is an intriguing old woman who is psychologizing me, and is using the Master's name simply to play on my credulity and force me to do what she wants. Here will be a good opportunity for me to show that I can keep my will free and preserve my independence of action. Thus I took no steps in the matter. But I had reason to repent this later on, for I discovered that had I offered my estate for sale at that time I could have sold it most advantageously, also that my son would have raised no objection, in fact he urged my selling it, which I did, eventually, a few years later, at a considerable loss, after having had much worry and annoyance about it in the meantime.

I have related this incident to show that H.P.B. did not coerce me in any way. I have often heard it said that those who lived with H.P.B. were mere puppets in her hands, and that she hypnotised them and forced them to do whatever suited her best. Now this is a clear proof to the contrary in my case, and, though I had to suffer for it at the time, I am glad to be able to show how my mistrusting the Master's word through H.P.B. was exceedingly unwise. Experience teaches one to be humble, for later knowledge proves the many errors in judgment we fall into during life, and in looking back over the years spent with H.P.B. I feel how much I lost by not understanding, or fully appreciating, her mission in life, as I do now.

It is my one continual regret that I lost so much of that precious time by not comprehending either her position or my own. But when I first went to her I was a woman of the world, one who had been a petted child of fortune. Through my husband's political position I occupied a prominent place in society; it therefore took me a long time to realise the hollowness of what I had hitherto looked upon as being the most desirable objects in life, and it required much training and many a hard battle with myself before I could conquer the satisfaction in self which a life of idleness, ease, and high position is sure to engender. So much had to be "knocked out of me," to use one of H.P.B.'s own phrases, and it is with a feeling of intense gratitude that I look back on the past, and think of all she did for me, and how she rendered me a slightly better instrument for the work in the Theosophical Society which it is both my duty and my pleasure to perform.

All who have known and loved H.P.B. have felt what a charm there was about her, how truly kind and loveable she was; at times such a bright childish nature seemed to beam around her, and a spirit of joyous fun would sparkle in her whole countenance, and cause the most winning expression that I have ever seen on a human face. One f the marvels of her character was, that to everybody she was different. I have never seen her treat two persons alike. The weak traits in everyone's character were known to her at once, and the extraordinary way in which she would probe them was surprising. By those who lived in daily contact with her the knowledge of *Self* was gradually acquired, and by those who chose to benefit by her practical way of teaching progress could be made. But to many of her pupils the process was unpalatable, for it is never pleasant to be brought face to face with one's own weaknesses; and so many turned from her, but those who could stand the test, and remain true to her, would recognise within themselves the inner development which alone leads to Occultism. A truer and more faithful friend one could never have than H.P.B., and I think it the greatest blessing of my life to have lived with her in such close intimacy, and until my death I shall try and further the noble cause for which she slaved and suffered so much.

I have been lingering on many points which have nothing directly to do with the writing of *The Secret Doctrine*; but it seems to me that by showing some of the details of H.P.B.'s life at that time, one gains a better comprehension of the woman who wrote that stupendous work. Day after day she would sit there writing through all the long hours, and nothing could be more monotonous and wearisome than her life regarded from an outside point of view. But, I suppose, at that time she lived much in the inner world, and there saw sights and visions which compensated for the dreariness of her daily life. She had, however, a distraction of rather a peculiar nature. In front of her writing table, attached to the wall, was a cuckoo clock, and this used to behave in a very extraordinary manner.

Sometimes it would strike like a loud gong, then sigh and groan as if possessed, cuckooing in the most unexpected way. Our maid, Louise, who was the most dense and apathetic of mortals, was very much afraid of it, and told us solemnly one day that she thought the devil was in it. "Not that I believe in the devil," she said, "but this cuckoo almost speaks to me at times." And so it did. One evening I went into the room and saw what appeared to me like streams of electric light coming out of the clock in all directions. On telling H.P.B. she replied, " Oh, it is only the spiritual telegraph, they are laying it on stronger to-night on account of to-morrow's work." Living in this atmosphere and coming into contact so continually with these, usually unseen, forces, this all seemed the true reality to me, and the outer world was that which appeared vague and unsatisfactory.

Frequent mention has been made here of H.P.B.'s Master, and I think that it will be interesting to some of my readers to hear how she first became acquainted with her Teacher.

During her childhood she had often seen near her an Astral form, that always seemed to come in any moment of danger, and save her just at the critical point. H.P.B. had learnt to look upon this Astral form as a guardian angel, and felt that she was under His care and guidance.

When she was in London, in 1851, with her father, Colonel Hahn, she was one day out walking when, to her astonishment, she saw a tall Hindu in the street with some Indian princes. She immediately recognised him as the same person that she had seen in the Astral. Her first impulse was to rush forward to speak to him, but he made her a sign not to move, and she stood as if spellbound while he passed on. The next day she went into Hyde Park for a stroll, that she might be alone and free to think over her extraordinary adventure. Looking up, she saw the same form approaching her, and then her Master told her that he had come to London with the Indian princes on an important mission, and he was desirous of meeting her personally, as he required her co-operation in a work which he was about to undertake. He then told her how the Theosophical Society was to be formed, and that he wished her to be the founder. He gave her a slight sketch of all the troubles she would have to undergo, and also told her that she would have to spend three years in Tibet to prepare her for the important task.

After three days' serious consideration and consultation with her father, H.P.B. decided to accept the offer made to her and shortly afterwards left London for India.

In Würzburg a curious incident occurred. Madame Fadeef—H.P.B.'s aunt—wrote to her that she was sending a box to the Ludwigstrasse containing what seemed to her a lot of rubbish. The box arrived, and to me was deputed the task of unpacking it. As I took out one thing after another and passed them to Madame Blavatsky, I heard her give an exclamation of delight, and she said, " Come and look at this which I wrote in the year 1851, the day I saw my blessed Master ; " and there in a scrap book in faded writing, I saw a few lines in which H.P.B. described the above interview. This scrap-book we still have in our possession. I copy the lines :

" Nuit memorable   Certaine nuit par un clair de lune qui se couchait à—Ramsgate,* 12 Août,† 1851—lorsque je rencontrai le Maître de mes rêves."

I was in England at the time of the visit of the Indians, and remember hearing that they and their suite were a fine set of men and one of them immensely tall.

Col. Olcott in his *Old Diary Leaves* for June, 1893, writes :—

" I had ocular proof that at least some of those who worked with us were living men, from having seen them in the flesh in India, after having seen them in the Astral body in America and in Europe; from having touched and talked with them. Instead of telling me that they were spirits, they told me they were as much alive as myself, and that each of them had his own peculiarities and capabilities, in short, his complete individuality They told me that what they had attained to I should one day myself acquire, how soon would depend entirely upon myself; and that I might anticipate nothing whatever from favour, but, like them, must gain every step, every inch of progress by my own exertions.

---

*On seeing the manuscript I asked why she had written " Ramsgate ' instead of " London," and H.P.B. told me that it was a blind, so that anyone casually taking up her book would not know where she had met her Master, and that her first interview with him had been in London as she had previously told me,.

" † Le 12 Août—c'est Juillet 31 style russe—jour de ma naissance —*vingt ans !* "

CHAPTER IX.

But the winter sped by, and the spring came on, and one morning H.P.B. received a letter from a friend of several years' standing, one of the oldest members of the society, Miss Kislingbury, who wrote that she would come and pay us a visit. We were delighted at the prospect, and hailed with pleasure the arrival of the companion of former days, who, having read the malignant attack of the Society for Psychical Research on H.P.B., could not rest till she came to assure her friend of her unabated affection and loyalty, and of her just indignation at the unfair and preposterous charges brought against her. The day passed swiftly in hearing all the news from the outside world and in discussing the Theosophical Society generally. At this time, too, we received a visit from Mr. and Madame Gebhard. They were both in great trouble, having lately lost a dearly loved son, and they received a warm and welcome greeting from H.P.B. and myself. They had been such true and kind friends that their visit to Würzburg was like a ray of sunlight to us. As we were now in full spring it was time to think of our summer plans and H.P.B. decided to spend the ensuing summer months at Ostend with her sister and niece.

Madame Gebhard was anxious to make a short stay in Austria and persuaded me to accompany her to Kempten, a very lonely place surrounded by lovely scenery. But its great charm and attraction for us lay in the fact that it was a town renowned for its haunted houses and the many occultists who resided there. Dr. Franz Hartmann was there, and as we thought that we should like to become better acquainted with him, we made our plans, and began the arduous task of packing. In a few days all H.P.B.'s boxes were corded and locked and the eventful journey was about to begin. Miss Kislingbury was returning to London, and kindly promised to accompany H.P.B. as far as Ostend. At Cologne they were to rest for a day or two and then proceed on their journey. Mr. Gebhard had promised to go and see them in Cologne, and as his daughter lived in that town we felt that Miss Kislingbury and H.P.B. would be well cared for.

It was always a formidable thing for H. P. B. to travel, and I looked in dismay at the nine packages which were to be placed inside her railway carriage. We started very early to go to the station, and there we seated H. P. B., surrounded by her numerous belongings, while we tried to make arrangements with the conductor to let her be alone in the compartment with Miss Kislingbury and her maid, Louise. After much discussion and protestation he opened the door of a carriage for us, and then began the serious task of piling up all the baggage, consisting of pillows, coverlets, handbags, and the precious box containing the manuscript of *The Secret Doctrine*: this was never to be out of her sight. Well, poor H. P. B., who had not been out of her room for weeks, had to walk all along the platform, and this was performed with difficulty. We got her comfortably settled, and were just rejoicing to think that the onerous task was satisfactorily completed, when one of the officials came to the door and began to remonstrate violently against the carriage being crowded with packages. He talked in German, H. P. B. answered in French, and I began to wonder how it would all end, when, fortunately, the whistle was heard and the train began to move out of the station. A feeling of pity came over me for Miss Kislingbury, as a vision of all these packages having to be taken out of the train at Cologne came upon me, and I felt what a responsibility was hers.

A few hours later I was on the road towards the south with Mme. Gebhard. The days of our companionship sped by swiftly and pleasantly, and then we parted, she going to Wiesbaden and I returning to Sweden to spend the summer in my own home. The first news I had of H. P. B. was that the day after she and Miss Kislingbury arrived in Cologne, Mr. Gebhard with several members of his family persuaded her to go and pay them a visit in Elberfeld. Miss Kislingbury returned to London and Madame Blavatsky went to the house of her kind friends.

During the summer months I frequently received letters from H. P. B., and the first news was of a sad nature. She had fallen on the slippery parquet of the Gebhard's house in Elberfeld and had unfortunately sprained her ankle and hurt her leg. This naturally prevented her from carrying out her plan of continuing her journey to Ostend; she remained, therefore, with her friends, whose kindness was unbounded. They omitted nothing that might alleviate her sufferings and make life pleasant to her. To this end they invited Mme. Jelihowsky with her daughter to stay with them, and H. P. B. was glad to have her relatives with her once more. In one letter she writes:—

"My old leg goes a little better, pain gone, but it is entirely helpless, and heaven alone knows *when* I will be able to walk with it even as superficially as I did before. Dear kind Mrs. Gebhard! she *does* nurse me, and is kind enough to find that I am a great deal better tempered than I used to be before! *Et pour cause.* There are no traitors in the field as there were then. . . . .

"Manuscript of *The Secret Doctrine* come back from our Revd. friend; he finds it far superior to the introductory—but not even half-a-dozen words corrected. He says it is *perfect.*"

As nearly all these letters from H. P. B. are concerned with the welfare of the Theosophical Society through the various personalities composing it, I find it almost impossible to quote from her letters without bringing in portions concerning the prominent members of that time, and as I have tried in these notes to avoid touching on personalities as much as I can, I only quote a few occasional sentences.

On her arrival in Ostend with her sister and niece, she writes :—

"Here I am—sad disenchantment all in all. Had I known what I know now, I would have remained quiet in Würzburg and gone to Kissingen and left the latter only in September, but such is, and was, my fate, and it was decreed that I should spend all my poor savings and pass the winter in Ostend. Now it's done and there is no help for it. The Hotels (ye gods of Avitchi!). For one night at the *Continental* I had to pay 117 francs for our rooms. Then in despair my sister rose in the morning and felt herself drawn to a certain part of the Boulevard on the sea shore, and in a side street she found an apartment with a whole *rez de chaussée* to let, three splendid rooms on the left and two on the right of the passage, or five rooms and a kitchen downstairs, the whole for 1000 francs for the season, and 100 francs a month afterwards, so what could I do? Result your legless friend established in a suite of rooms on the left, and my sister has two rooms, a bedroom, an elegant one, and a parlour or dining room on the right side of the passage. When she goes away, which will, be in ten days that, suite remains empty. But then, perhaps Mr. Sinnett will come. It is nice to have two such rooms for one's friends. As for myself I have lovely rooms, bedroom running by a separated arch and satin hangings into a large study, and a small drawing-room with a piano in it near by. I have the whole floor to myself.

"Yes, I will try and settle once more at my *Secret Doctrine*. But it is hard. I am very weak, dear, I feel so poorly and legless as I never did when you were there to care for me. . . . . I am as nervous as a she-cat, I feel I am ungrateful. But then, it is because gratitude has ever been shown in ancient symbology to reside in people's heels, and having lost my legs how can I be expected to have any? I have affection—but only for . . ."

Later on :—

"I am trying to write *The Secret Doctrine*. But Sinnett, who is here for a few days, wants all my attention directed to the blessed Memoirs. Mrs. Sinnett was unable to come, and he wil soon leave me, and thus I shall be left legless, friendless and alone with my karma. Pretty *tête-à-tête !* "

From another letter :—

" My poor legs have parted company with my body. It is a limitless if not an eternal 'furlong,' as they say in India. Whatever the cause may be, I am now as legless as any elemental can be. No, except Louise and my landlady with her cat and robin I do not know a soul in Ostend. Not one solitary Russian here this season except myself, who would rather be a Turk and go back to India. But I can't, for I have neither legs nor reputation according to the infamous charges of the S. P. R. . . . . I think the gout and rheumatism will soon reach the heart, I feel great pain in it."

Poor H. P. B.! she suffered terribly at that time. She was so anxious to get on with her writing, and the continual obstacles which came in her way were very trying to her. In all her letters she urged me to return to her, for she felt that with me near her she would be free from many petty annoyances, and also that the calm and quiet that were absolutely necessary to her in writing *The Secret Doctrine* would be ensured to her. I was glad when the day came that I could return to her side, and our meeting was a very joyful one : there was so much to tell on both sides. It pained me to see that H.P.B. was suffering more than when she left Würzburg, but she told me that she had found an intelligent doctor in Ostend, and that she had made an arrangement for him to come and see her every week.

We soon settled down to our routine life, and I was thankful to see that with every day H.P.B. was able to do more work and was getting into what she called her "currents" again. The communications from her Master and from the different chelâs were frequent, and we lived entirely in a world of our own. But Ostend was more easy of access than Würzburg, and visitors began to break the monotony of our existence. Two of our members came from Paris and stayed a fortnight with us. These were Messrs. Gaboriau and Coulomb, and the evenings were passed in asking H.P.B. questions, which she answered with readiness, reading out to them, here and there, passages from *The Secret Doctrine* which she had written during the day. Mr. Eckstein, from Vienna, paid us a short visit, also Mr. Arthur Gebhard, who was on his way to Germany from America, where he had spent several years, and H.P.B. was eager to hear all the Theosophical news from that country.

One day H.P.B. called me and asked me whether I could go to London to undertake some private business of her own. I told her that I would willingly do so, but felt anxious about leaving her alone. So I started for London with a heavy heart, as I thought of the old lady's loneliness and her look of sad yearning as she gave me a farewell kiss.

I received frequent letters from H.P.B. while in London, and the following are a few extracts taken from them:—

" I am wretched because with every day more the conviction is growing stronger in me that there is not a corner on this earth where I could be left to live and die quietly. Because I have no home, no one I could rely on implicitly, because there is no one *able to understand me* thoroughly and the position I am placed in. Because, ever since you went away, I am pestered by the police—cautiously, true, with great prudence so far, but quite clearly enough for me to see I am regarded with suspicion even in that affair of a million stolen on the railway between Ostend and Brussels!!! Three times they have been asking after *you* to give them information, and twice a man from the police came to me asking my name before and after marriage, my age, where I came from, where I last lived, when I came to Würzburg, to Elberfield, etc. Two days ago they came after Louise and demanded that she should go with them to the police station and they asked her many questions. Finally, do what I may, all turns out *an evil* for me, and all is misconstrued and misinterpreted by my best friends, that I am traduced, slandered, not by strangers, but by those who were, or seemed to be, most attached to me, and whom I loved really. . . Because lies, hypocrisy and jesuitism reign supreme in the world and that I am not and cannot be either, therefore I seem doomed. Because I am tired of life and the struggles of that stone of Sisyphus and the eternal work of the Danaides—and that I am not permitted to get out of this misery and rest. Because whether I am right or wrong I am *made out wrong*. Because I am *one too many* on this earth, that's all."

Again :—

" Remember much as I need you (and I need you badly), as

I know through Master that you are doing excellent work in London, please stay a week or more even if you think it right, I feel very miserable, but I can stand it, never mind. Z. is very young and never gets up till 12 or 1 o'clock, but he is doing me good service, finding me a few quotations and correcting the English in some of the appendices."

Just before leaving Würzburg, H.P.B. had sent her manuscripts for *The Secret Doctrine* to Adyar to Col. H. S. Olcott, the President of the Society. She was anxious to have his opinion as he had helped her so much with *Isis*. She also wished the manuscript to be submitted to Mr. Subba Row, and the few pages which he had read interested him so much that he was anxious to see more. H.P.B. wrote to me on this subject :—

"I sent a telegram yesterday asking whether I could send you to London my MSS., as I have to forward it without delay to Madras. It is all splendidly packed up by Louise's husband, corded and sewn in oil cloth, all secure for the journey, so you will have no trouble with it, but to have it insured. Please do this yourself. You are the only one in whom I have absolute faith. Olcott writes that Subba Row is so anxious about the MSS. that he is enquiring daily when it comes, etc., and Master ordered him, it appears, to look it over. Please send it on by this mail and do insure it for no less than £150 or £200, for if lost—well good-bye!—so I send it to you to-day to your address and do answer immediately you receive it."

An extract from another letter :—

"After a long conversation with Master—the first for a long, long time—I have acquired two convictions. 1st, the T.S. was ruined for having been transplanted on the European soil. Had only Master's philosophy been given and phenomena been kept in the background it would have been a success. These accursed phenomena have ruined my character which is a small thing and welcome, but they have also ruined Theosophy in Europe. In India it will live and prosper. 2nd conviction! the whole Society (Europe and America) is under cruel probation. Those who come out of it unscathed will have their reward. Those who will remain inactive or passive, even as those who will turn their backs, will have theirs also. It is a final and supreme trial. But there is news. Either I have to return to India to die this autumn, or I have to form between this and November next a nucleus of true Theosophists, a school of my own, with no secretary, only myself alone, with as many mystics as I can get to teach them. I can stop here, or go to England, or whatever I like. . . . You say literature is the only salvation. Well, see the good effect Mme. Blavatsky's Memoirs have produced. Seven or eight French papers pitching into Sinnett, myself, K. H., etc., on account of these Memoirs. A true revival of Theosophical Society scandals over again, just because of this literature. If phenomena were thrown overboard and philosophy alone stuck to, then, says Master, the T.S. could be saved in Europe. But phenomena are the curse and ruin of the Society. Because I wrote twice or thrice to Z. telling him what he did and thought and read on such and such a day, he is crazy and a full-blown mystic. Well, may the Master inspire and protect you, for you have to play a part in the coming struggle. I hear the people who subscribed to *The Secret Doctrine* are getting impatient—cannot be helped. I, *you know*, work fourteen hours a day. The last MSS. sent to Adyar will not be back for three months, but then we can begin publishing. Subba Row is making valuable notes, so Olcott tells me. I am not going to move from the neighbourhood of, or from, England itself. *Here is my place* in Europe and that's settled. Within easy reach of London is the programme given and I shall stick to it. I wish to goodness you would come back quicker. Your room upstairs with stove is ready, so you will be more comfortable. But you do useful work in London. I feel as lonely as I can be——"

Again :—

"Only a few words, since, thank goodness, I will see you again soon. Say to those who have asked you, 'My Master is a white Magician and a Mahâtmâ too. There can be no Mahâtmâ who is not a white Magician, whether he exercises his power or not, though not every Magician can reach Mahâtmâship, which state is positively like the metaphor used by Mohini, for the state of Mahâtmâship *dissolves man's physical nature*, intellect, feeling of the Ego, and all except the body, like a piece of sugar in water. But supposing even my Master was not yet a full Mahâtmâ, which no one can say but Himself and the other Mahâtmâs near Him, what difference does that make to anyone? f he is no better than the three Magi (white Magicians, who came from the East to see the birth of Christ) I am quite satisfied. To end, let those who trouble you learn the etymology of the word Magician. It comes from *Mah, Maha, Mag*, identical with the root of the word Mahâtmâ. One means great soul, *Mah-âtmâ*, the other great worker, *Mahansa* or *Maghusha*. Mohini is right to instruct people and give them the true definition between the *states* of the man who belongs to this state. Those who fall into it occasionally are Mahâtmâs just as much as any. Those in whom that state becomes *permanent* are that 'piece of sugar'; they can no longer concern themselves with the things of this world. They are 'Jivanmuktas!'

"Ever since you went away, I have felt as though either paralysis or a split in the heart would occur. I am as cold as ice and four doses of *digitalis* in one day could not quiet the heart. Well, let me only finish my *Secret Doctrine*. Last night, instead of going to bed I was made to write till 1 o'clock. The *triple Mystery* is given out—one I had thought they would never have given out—that of. . ."

I felt very anxious after receiving this letter. I hurried through the remaining work as quickly as possible, and was much distressed on arriving at Ostend to find H.P.B. looking so worn and ill. Mr. Z. soon left, and then we recommenced our usual routine of life, and the writing of *The Secret Doctrine* was carried on strenuously. Very rarely was I able to persuade H.P.B. to go in a bath chair on the esplanade. I thought that the warmth from the sun and the sea air might do her good, but she always seemed dissatisfied when she came in, as if she felt she had done wrong in losing so much valuable time. She used often to say: " Soon we shall no longer be alone, and then the conditions will be altered, and the currents will be broken, and I shall not be able to work nearly so well." And so she would keep at her desk, no matter what her pains or sufferings were. She just clenched her teeth together and fought her battle bravely.

CHAPTER X.

ONE day we were agreeably surprised by a visit from Mrs. Kingsford and Mr. Maitland. They were in Ostend for a few days on their way to Paris, and were staying at an hotel opposite our house. As Mrs. Kingsford complained much of the discomforts of this hotel, and as she seemed to be in very delicate health, both H.P.B. and I proposed that she and Mr. Maitland should become our guests. I gave up my room to Mrs. Kingsford, and they spent a fortnight with us. Both ladies were usually occupied with their respective work during the day-time, but in the evenings delightful conversations ensued, and it was interesting to me to hear different points of *The Secret Doctrine* discussed from the Eastern and Western standpoints of occultism. The powerful intellects of these two gifted women would be engaged in animated discussions, starting from apparently two opposite poles. Gradually the threads of their conversation would seem to approach each other, until at last they would merge in one unity. Fresh topics would then arise which would be grappled with in the same masterly way. But these delightful evenings soon drew to a close, for Mrs. Kingsford became very ill and was not able to leave her room, and Mr. Maitland thought it expedient to take her to a warmer climate, so one fine morning they started for Paris and H.P.B. and I were once more alone.

Letters now came to us frequently from London, and we heard with pleasure that some slight activity was beginning to be shewn there. A London group for study had been formed, and most of the members seemed very earnest and were continually writing for information and guidance; indeed, things seemed going on more favourably in that direction, and H.P.B. was pleased to think that there was some activity in that quarter.

To my great distress, I now began to notice that she became drowsy and heavy in the middle of the day, and often was unable to work for an hour together. This increased rapidly, and as the doctor who attended her pronounced it to be an affection of the kidneys, I became alarmed, and sent a telegram to Madame Gebhard to tell her of my apprehensions, and to beg her to come and help me. I felt that the responsibility was too great for me to cope with alone. I had also tried getting a nurse to help me with the night work, but it was only possible to find a *sœur de charité*, and I soon discovered that she was worse than useless, for whenever my back was turned she was holding up her crucifix before H.P.B., and entreating her to come into the fold of the only church before it was too late. This nearly drove H.P.B. wild. I therefore sent this nurse away, and no other being available, I hired a cook, and this set Louise free to devote more attention to H.P.B.; but, as Louise's little girl had been sent to her only a few weeks previously from Switzerland, I found that even her help was not very valuable, as her child occupied all her thoughts. I was, therefore, thankful when I received a cordial response to my telegram and knew that in a few hours I should see Madame Gebhard.

When she came I felt as if a great burden had been lifted off my shoulders. In the meanwhile H.P.B. was getting worse, and the Belgian doctor, who was kindness itself, tried one remedy after another, but with no good result, and I began to get seriously alarmed and anxious as to what course I should adopt. H.P.B. was in a heavy lethargic state, she seemed to be unconscious for hours together, and nothing could rouse or interest her. Finally a bright inspiration came to me. In the London group I knew there was a Doctor Ashton Ellis, so I telegraphed to him, described the state that H.P.B. was in, and entreated him to come without delay.

I sat by H.P.B.'s bed that night listening to every sound as I anxiously watched the hours go by, till at last, at 3 a.m., the joyful sound of a bell was heard. I flew to the door, opened it, and the doctor walked in. I eagerly told him all her symptoms, and described the remedies that had been applied, whereupon he went to her and made her drink some medicine that he had brought with him. Then, after giving me a few directions, he retired to his room to get a few hours' rest. I told Madame Gebhard of the doctor's arrival, and finally returned to my post.

The next day there was a consultation between the two doctors. The Belgian doctor said that he had never known a case of a person with the kidneys attacked as H.P.B.'s were, living as long as she had done, and that he was convinced that nothing could save her. He held out no hope of her recovery. Mr. Ellis replied that it was exceedingly rare for anyone to survive so long in such a state. He further told us that he had consulted a specialist before coming to Ostend who was of the same opinion, but advised that, in addition to the prescribed medicine, he should try massage, so as to stimulate the paralysed organs.

Madame Gebhard suggested that, as H.P.B. was so near death, she ought to make her will, for if she died intestate in a foreign country there would be no end of confusion and annoyance about her property, as she had no relations near her. She added that she had already consulted with H.P.B., who had told her that she was willing to sign a will, that she wished all her property to be left to me, and that she would give me private directions how I was to dispose of it. Later on H.P.B. told me exactly what I was to do with her property, which, however, amounted to but little—consisting only of her clothes, a few books, some jewelry, and a few pounds in cash; but still it was thought advisable that the will should be made, and the lawyer, the two doctors, and the American consul, were to be present.

The night passed quietly, and several times the following day Mr. Ellis massé'd her until he was quite exhausted; but she got no better, and to my horror I began to detect that peculiar faint odour of death which sometimes precedes dissolution. I hardly dared hope that she would live through the night, and while I was sitting alone by her bedside she opened her eyes and told me how glad she was to die, and that she thought the Master would let her be free at last. Still she was very anxious about her *Secret Doctrine*. I must be most careful of her manuscripts and hand all over to Col. Olcott with directions to have them printed. She had hoped that she would have been able to give more to the world, but the Master knew best. And so she talked on at intervals, telling me many things. At last she dropped off into a state of unconsciousness, and I wondered how it would all end.

It seemed to me impossible that she should die and leave her work unfinished; and then, again, the Theosophical Society . . . . what would become of it ? How could it be that the Master who was at the head of that Society should allow it to crumble away. True, it might be the outcome of the Karma of the members, who through their false-heartedness and faint-heartedness had brought the Theosophical Society to such a point that there was no more vitality in it, and so it had to die out, only to be revived in the course of the next century. Still the thought came to me that the Master had told H. P. B. that she was to form a circle of students around her and that she was to teach them. How could she do that if she were to die ? And then I opened my eyes and glanced at her and thought, was it possible that she who had slaved, suffered and striven so hard should be allowed to die in the middle of her work ? What would be the use of all her self-sacrifice and the agony she had gone through if the work of her life was not to be completed ? Day after day she had suffered tortures, both of mind and body : of mind through the falsity and treachery of those who had called themselves friends and then had slandered her behind her back, casting stones at her while they in their ignorance thought she would never know the hand that had thrown them; and of the body, because she was compelled to remain in a form which should have disintegrated two years previously in Adyar, if it had not been held together by occult means when she decided to live on and work for those who were still to come into the Theosophical Society. None of those who knew her, really understood her. Even to me, who had been alone with her for so many months, she was an enigma, with her strange powers, her marvellous knowledge, her extraordinary insight into human nature, and her mysterious life, spent in regions unknown to ordinary mortals, so that though her body might be near, her soul was often away in commune with others. Many a time have I observed her thus and known that only the shell of her body was present.

Such were the thoughts which passed through my mind, as I sat hour after hour that anxious night, watching her as she seemed to be getting weaker and weaker. A wave of blank despondency came over me, as I felt how truly I loved this noble woman, and I realised how empty life would be without her. No longer to have her affection and her confidence would be a most severe trial. My whole soul rose in rebellion at the thought of losing her, . .

. . . .

I gave a bitter cry and knew no more.

When I opened my eyes, the early morning light was stealing in, and a dire apprehension came over me that I had slept, and that perhaps H. P. B. had died during my sleep—died whilst I was untrue to my vigil. I turned round towards the bed in horror, and there I saw H. P. B. looking at me calmly with her clear grey eyes, as she said, " Countess, come here." I flew to her side. " What has happened, H. P. B.—you look so different to what you did last night." She replied, " Yes, Master has been here; He gave me my choice, that I might die and be free if I would, or I might live and finish *The Secret Doctrine*. He told me how great would be my sufferings and what a terrible time I would have before me in England (for I am to go there); but when I thought of those students to whom I shall be permitted to teach a few things, and of the Theosophical Society in general, to which I have already given my heart's blood, I accepted the sacrifice, and now to make it complete, fetch me some coffee and something to eat, and give me my tobacco box."

I flew off to do her errands and ran to tell Madame Gebhard the good news. I found her just dressed, ready to relieve me from my night's watchings, and after several joyous exclamations she insisted on my going to bed while she attended on H.P.B herself. I felt so excited that I thought that I should nèver sleep again, but my head was no sooner on the pillow than I was in a deep slumber, and I did not wake till late in the day.

When I came down all was joy. H.P.B. was up and dressed, talking merrily to us all. Mr. Ellis had again massé'd her and given her medicine, and all were awaiting the arrival of the party who were to come and superintend the making of the will. H.P.B. was in the dining room ready to receive them, and they looked aghast with astonishment, as they came in with long and serious faces expecting to be shown into the presence of a dying woman. The doctor was beside himself. He said, "*Mais, c'est inoui; Madame, aurait dû mourir.*" He could not make it out, H.P.B. seated on her chair, smoking her cigarette, quietly offered him one and then began chaffing him. The lawyer was puzzled and turned to the Belgian doctor for an explanation. The other began excusing himself, repeating several times, "*Mais elle aurait dû mourir,*" when the American Consul, like a man of the world, came forward, shook hands with H.P.B. and told her that he was delighted that she had cheated death this time, and an animated and amusing conversation ensued.

Then the lawyer called us all to order and the serious task of making the will began. H.P.B. was asked to give details about her husband, but she broke forth:—She knew nothing about old Blavatsky, he was probably dead long ago, and they had better go to Russia if they wanted to know anything about him ; she had asked them to come there to make her will. She was supposed to be dying and now she was not going to die, but as they were present it was a pity that they should have come for nothing, so they might make the will all the same and she would leave everything to me.

The lawyer now expostulated. Had she no relations ; would it not be right to leave her property to them ? And then he looked askance at me, as if he thought that I might have been unduly influencing H.P.B. to leave her money to me to the detriment of her relatives. H.P.B. flew out at him, and asked him what business it was of his; she should leave her money, she declared, to whom she chose. Madame Gebhard, fearful of a scene, interposed and said gently to the lawyer :— " Perhaps, when you know the amount which Madame Blavatsky has to will away, you will have no further objections to making the will as she desires ; for had Madame Blavatsky died there would not have been sufficient money to pay for her funeral expenses."

The lawyer could not restrain an expression of surprise, but set to work without further comment. In a few minutes the will was made and signed by those present, then coffee was served and a general talk followed. After three hours had passed the American Consul got up and said: " Well, I think this is enough fatigue for a dying woman," and so with a few flying compliments the little party left the room, while we who remained enjoyed a hearty laugh at one of the most original and amusing scenes we had ever witnessed. We then thought that H.P.B. ought to go to bed, but she rebelled most vigorously and sat there till a late hour playing her " patiences."

I will add a few words here to say that I never saw that will again. After H.P.B.'s death in Avenue Road, London, on the eighth of May, 1891, I went to Ostend to see the lawyer and ask him what had been done with the will. He told me that after my departure he had given the will to H.P.B., and I suppose that she must have destroyed the deed, as it was never found among her papers.

The excitement attendant on H.P.B.'s recovery gradually subsided. Mr. Ellis returned to London, carrying with him our most grateful thanks for his kindness in responding so readily to my telegram, and for the care and devotion which he showed to H.P.B. during his stay with us. Our next visitors were Dr. Keightley and Mr. Bertram Keightley. They came bearing with them the most pressing and warm invitations from the London group to H.P.B. to come and live in England. This she finally consented to do, and it was agreed that she should spend the summer with the Keightleys at Norwood in a small house called Maycot.

They returned to London to make preparations for her reception and I began to turn my thoughts to my home in Sweden. I felt thoroughly tired out with all the anxiety I had lately gone through, and I longed for complete rest, both bodily and mental. Madame Gebhard, seeing how worn and ill I looked, urged me to go at once, saying that she would stay with H.P.B. until the Keightleys came to fetch her, and as that morning a letter had been received from Mr. Thornton, telling us that he was coming to Ostend to pay H.P.B. a visit, I was glad to feel that Madame Gebhard would not be quite alone, but would have a friend to help her in case of need. Therefore, a few days later, after the tenderest and kindest of farewells, I found myself speeding away in the train for Sweden.

Beyond occasional letters from Madame Gebhard, telling me that all was going on satisfactorily and that they were busy packing and preparing for H.P.B.'s journey to London, there is nothing of importance to relate. During the summer I received occasional letters from H.P.B., and I here make extracts from two of them dated from Maycot, Norwood.

"I can only say that I do not feel happy or even *à mon aise* as I did at Ostend. I am in the enemy's camp, and this says all... This house is a hole where we are like herrings in a barrel—so small, so uncomfortable, and when there are three people in my two rooms (half the size of my Ostend bedroom), we tread uninterruptedly on each other's corns; when there are four, we sit on each other's heads. Then there is no quiet here, for the slightest noise is heard all over the house. It is personal trouble all this, but there is another one far more important. There is so much work here to do (Theosophical) that I have either to give up my *Secret Doctrine* or leave the Theosophical work undone. It is for this your presence is required more than anything. If we miss the good opportunities, we will never have better ones. You know, I suppose, that a Blavatsky Lodge was organised and legalized by Sinnett and all.

"It is composed of fourteen persons so far. You know also that a Theosophical Publishing Company has been formed by the same persons, and that not only have we started a new Theosophical Journal, but they insist on publishing themselves *The Secret Doctrine*. £200 down has been subscribed for *Lucifer*, our new journal, and £500 for *The Secret Doctrine*. It is a Limited Publishing Co., and already signed and legally registered. So much is done therefore. I have regular Thursday meetings, when ten or eleven people have to crowd into my two rooms, and sit on my writing table and sofa bed. I sleep on my Würzburg sofa, for there is no room for a bed. You, if you come, would have a room upstairs."

Further she wrote to me that the latest project was to take a house in London, the expenses to be shared by the two Keightleys, herself and myself, and hoped that I would agree to the plan, as she thought that it would be a great advantage to have a Theosophical Headquarters in London. It would facilitate our work considerably, and would induce others to come and see us more readily. Having written to tell her of my willingness to join in the proposed scheme and that she would see me in London, I received the following lines from her from Maycot :—

"To say how relieved and glad I am of your arrival is useless. Do come, and direct here for a few hours if you do not want to sleep here. The house in Lansdowne Road is being furnished. I am migrating, books and all. I have chosen two rooms for you, which I think you will like, *but do come and do not put off for mercy's sake.* Yours ever, H.P.B."

This is the last letter I shall quote from, and with this nearly ends my story, for in London it was the two Keightleys who worked at *The Secret Doctrine* with H.P.B. With praiseworthy diligence they wrote out the whole manuscript on a typewriting machine, and I leave it to them to continue the narrative of how H.P.B. wrote *The Secret Doctrine*. I will only add a few more lines.

I arrived in London in September, 1887, and went straight to Norwood; there I found H.P.B. in a tiny cottage with the Keightleys, and after receiving a warm welcome, she was eager to tell me how we were to begin work for the Theosophical Society in a more practical way than had hitherto been done. Many were the long talks we had as to how we could make Theosophy better known in London, and all sorts of projects were formed.

After three days spent in packing, planning, and arranging everything, we one morning got into a carriage and drove up to London, to 17, Lansdowne Road. There the two Keightleys were hard at work making the house comfortable for H. P. B. I could but admire, as I have since always done, the tender devotion and eager thought for her comfort, even down to trivial details, which these two young men have always shown. In every way they ever contributed to her well-being, trying by all available means to make the conditions easier for her to continue with her writing of *The Secret Doctrine*.

H. P. B.'s rooms were on the ground floor, a small bedroom leading into a large writing-room, where furniture was so arranged around her, that she could reach her books and papers without difficulty; and this room again led into the dining-room, so that she had ample space for exercise when she felt inclined to walk about.

It was here that Colonel Olcott found her a few months later, and described his impressions for his Indian readers. The passage* runs :—

"The President found Madame Blavatsky in bad health, but working with desperate and pertinacious energy. An able physician told him that the fact of her even being alive at all was in itself a miracle, judging by all professional canons. Her system is so disorganised by a complication of diseases of the gravest character that it is a simple wonder that she can keep up the struggle; any other being must have succumbed long ago. The miscroscope reveals enormous crystals of uric acid in her blood, and the doctors say that it is more than likely that one hot month in India would kill her. Nevertheless, not only does she live, but she works at her writing desk from morning to night, preparing 'copy' and reading proofs for *The Secret Doctrine*

* Supplement to *The Theosophist*, Oct. 1888, p. xviii.

F

and her London magazine *Lucifer*. Of her greatest work over three hundred pages of each of the two volumes were already printed when Col. Olcott arrived, and both volumes will probably appear this month. From all he heard from competent judges who had read the MS., the President was satisfied that *The Secret Doctrine* will surpass in merit and interest even *Isis Unveiled*.

"Madame Blavatsky is living at 17, Lansdowne Road, Holland Park, with three Theosophical friends, among them her devoted guardian, nurse and consoler, the Countess Wachtmeister of Sweden, who has attended her throughout all her serious illnesses of the past three years. The house is a pleasant one, in a quiet neighbourhood, and the back of it looks upon a small private park or compound common to the occupants of all the houses which surround it. Madame Blavatsky's rooms are on the ground floor, she being practically unable to go up or down stairs. Her desk faces a large window looking out upon the green grass and leafy trees of Holland Park; at her right and left hands are tables and book racks filled with books of reference; and all about the room are her Indian souvenirs—Benares bronzes, Palghat mats, Adoni carpets, Moradabad platters, Kashmir plaques, and Sinhalese images, which were so familiar to visitors at Adyar in the old days. As regards her return to India the question is largely a medical one. It is extremely doubtful whether she could stand the journey, and it is quite certain that she would have to be hoisted in and out of the steamer in a sling, as she was when she sailed from Madras for Europe, three years ago. Of course, with her book passing through the press, she could not quit London for a fortnight, even if she could arrange for the editorial conduct of *Lucifer*. Later on this obstacle will be out of the way, and it will remain a mere question of her health. Clustering around her in London she has several devoted Theosophists who, besides advancing £1,500 to bring out *The Secret Doctrine* and *Lucifer*, have formed a Theosophical Publishing Co., Ld., to issue at popular prices reprints of articles from *The Theosophist*, *Lucifer* and *The Path* and useful tracts of all sorts. The interest in Theosophy increases and deepens in Europe and still more in America; for not only do we see its ideas colouring current literature, bu provoking discussion by the first Orientalists of the day. The recent lectures of Professor Max Müller, Monier Williams, and others in which we are referred to and criticised, and the admirable article on 'Buddhism in the West,' by that learned scholar M. Em. Burnouf, which we have translated and printed in this issue of our magazine, illustrate the case very well. Practically there are now three Theosophical centres, whence influence of this kind is being exerted upon the mind of our age—Madras, London and New York. And however much Madame Blavatsky's absence from Adyar may be deplored by her ardent friends, it cannot be doubted that the movement as a whole profits by her presence in London, and her Theosophical proximity to our devoted colleagues in America."

In the following year another account appeared in *The Theosophist* for July, which may also be of interest to my readers:—

"Madame Blavatsky continues to labour as ceaselessly as ever, and under conditions of such physical disability as render not simply her working, but actually her living truly marvellous. I may say as a physician and not simply upon my own authority, but as a fact known to some of the leading medical practitioners of London, that never before has a patient been known to live even for a week under such conditions of renal disorder as have been chronic with her for very many months past. Lately they have been somewhat modified by the action of strychnia, of which she has taken a little over six grains daily. Very frequently she has attacks of cerebral apoplexy, but without any treatment known to medical science wards them off and goes on, firmly confident as ever that her present life will not end before its work is fully accomplished. And in that work she is indefatigable. Her hours of labour are daily from 6.30 a.m. to 7 p.m., with only a few minutes' interruption for a light meal just before the sun reaches the meridian. During that time she devotes a great deal of her time to preparing the instructions for the Esoteric Section, giving out such knowledge as is permitted her to impart and its members are capable of receiving. Then the editorial labour connected with the production of her magazine *Lucifer* devolves entirely upon her. And she also edits the new French Theosophical monthly magazine *La Revue Theosophique*, published by the Countess d'Adhemar, who, by the way, is an American by birth. Her magazine is now publishing a series of brilliant articles by Amaravella, and a translation in French of Madame Blavatsky's *Secret Doctrine*.

" The third volume of *The Secret Doctrine* is in MS. ready to be given to the printers. It will consist mainly of a series of sketches of the great Occultists of all ages, and is a most wonderful and fascinating work. The fourth volume, which is to be largely hints on the subject of practical Occultism, has been outlined but not yet written. It will demonstrate what Occultism really is, and show how the popular conception of it has been outraged and degraded by fraudulent pretenders to its mysteries, who have, for greed of gain or other base purposes, falsely claimed possession of the secret knowledge. This exposure will necessitate its being brought up sharply to date as a historical record, so that the actual work of writing it will not be commenced until we are about ready to bring it forth.

"In the evening, from 7 until 11 o'clock, and sometimes 2 o'clock a.m., Madame Blavatsky receives visitors, of whom she has many. Of course many are friends, others are serious investigators, and not a few are impelled by curiosity to see a woman who is one of the prominent personages of the world to-day. All are welcome, and she is equally ready in meeting all upon any ground they select.

"Mr. G. J. Romanes, a Fellow of the Royal Society, comes in to discuss the evolutionary theory set forth in her *Secret Doctrine;* Mr. W. T. Stead, editor of the *Pall Mall Gazette*, who is a great admirer of *The Secret Doctrine*, finds much in it that seems to invite further elucidation; Lord Crawford, Earl of Crawford and Balcarres, another F.R.S.—who is deeply interested in Occultism and Cosmogony, and who was a pupil of Lord Lytton and studied with him in Egypt—comes to speak of his special subjects of concern; Mrs. Besant, whose association with the National Reform Society has made her famous, drops in to express her interest in Theosophy as a power affecting the social life of humanity; Mr. Sidney Whitman, widely known by his scathing criticism upon English cant, has ideas to express and thoughts to interchange upon the ethics of Theosophy, and so they come."

A. K.

To return, we were hardly settled in the house before people began to call on H.P.B., and the visitors grew so numerous, and she was so constantly interrupted in her work, that it was considered advisable for her to have a day for reception. Saturday was chosen, and from 2 p.m. till 11 or 12 at night there would be a succession of visitors, and H.P.B. would frequently have a group around her asking questions, to which she would answer with unvarying patience. All this time *The Secret Doctrine* was being continued, until, at last, it was put into the printer's hands. Then began the task of proof-reading, revising, and correcting, which proved to be a very onerous one indeed. I watched it all with joy in my heart, and when a printed copy was put into my hands, I was thankful to feel that all these hours of pain, toil and suffering had not been in vain, and that H.P.B. had been able to accomplish her task and give to the world this grand book, which, she told me, would have to wait quietly until the next century to be fully appreciated, and would only be studied by the few now.

H.P.B. was happy that day. It was the one gleam of

sunshine amidst the darkness and dreariness of her life, for shadows were gathering round, and soon some of her bitterest trials were to be experienced.

But *The Secret Doctrine* finished, my task is done. Let me only add my small tribute of gratitude and love to the friend and teacher who did more for me than anybody in the world, who helped to show me the truth, and who pointed out to me the way to try and conquer self, with all its petty weaknesses, and to live more nobly for the use and good of others. " Thy soul has to become as the ripe mango fruit; as soft and sweet as its bright golden pulp for other's woes, as hard as that fruit's stone for thine own throes and sorrows.". . . " Compassion speaks and saith: can there be bliss when all that lives must suffer ? Shalt thou be saved and hear the whole world cry ? "* These are the precepts that H.P.B. bade her pupils learn and follow, these are the ethics that her life of continual self-abnegation for the good of others has set like a burning flame in the hearts of those that believed in her.

---

* From the *Voice of the Silence*.

APPENDIX I.

I.

Mr. BERTRAM KEIGHTLEY'S

ACCOUNT OF THE

WRITING OF "THE SECRET DOCTRINE."

The first I saw of *The Secret Doctrine* manuscript was on a visit paid to H.P.B. at Ostend, at the very beginning of the year 1887. I had gone over to urge upon H.P.B. the advisability of coming to settle in London for the purpose of forming a centre for active work in the cause of Theosophy. There were six of us in all who felt profoundly dissatisfied with the deadness which seemed to pervade the Society in England, and we had come to the conclusion that only H.P.B. could give efficient aid in restoring the suspended animation of the movement, and initiating active and wisely directed work. Of these six—with H.P.B. the original founders of the first Blavatsky Lodge—two only, alas! now remain active workers in the Society.

During the few days I then spent at Ostend with H.P.B., she asked me to look over parts of the MSS. of her new work, which I gladly consented to do. Before I had read much it grew plain that *The Secret Doctrine* was destined to be by far the most important contribution of this century to the literature of Occultism; though even then the in choate and fragmentary character of much of the work led me to think that careful revision and much re-arrangement would be needed before the manuscript would be fit for publication.

On a second visit a week or two later, this impression was confirmed by further examination; but as H.P.B. then consented to come and settle in or near London as soon as arrangements could be made for her reception, nothing further was done about it at the time.

Not long after my return to England we learnt that H.P.B. was seriously ill, in fact that her life was despaired of by the physicians in attendance. But, as usual, she disappointed the medical prophets and recovered with such marvellous rapidity that soon after we were able to make arrangements for her coming to England, to Upper Norwood, where a cottage, called Maycot, had been taken for her temporary residence.

The move was effected without any untoward event, though the packing up of her books, papers, MSS., etc., was a truly terrible undertaking, for she went on writing till the very last moment, and as sure as any book, paper, or portion of MSS. had been carefully packed away at the bottom of some box, so surely would she urgently need it, and insist upon its being disinterred at all costs. However, we did get packed at last, reached Maycot, and before we had been two hours in the house, H.P.B. had her writing materials out and was hard at work again. Her power of work was amazing; from early morning till late in the evening she sat at her desk, and even when so ill that most people would have been lying helpless in bed, she toiled resolutely away at the task she had undertaken.

A day or two after our arrival at Maycot, H.P.B.

placed the whole of the so-far completed MSS. in the hands of Dr. Keightley and myself, instructing us to read, punctuate, correct the English, alter, and generally treat it as if it were our own—which we naturally did *not* do, having far too high an opinion of her knowledge to take any liberties with so important a work.

But we both read the whole mass of MSS.—a pile over three feet high—most carefully through, correcting the English and punctuation where absolutely indispensable, and then, after prolonged consultation, faced the author in her den—in my case with sore trembling, I remember—with the solemn opinion that the whole of the matter must be re-arranged on some definite plan, since as it stood the book was another *Isis Unveiled*, only far worse, so far as absence of plan and consecutiveness were concerned.

After some talk, H.P.B. told us to go to Tophet and do what we liked. She had had more than enough of the blessed thing, had given it over to us, washed her hands thereof entirely, and we might get out of it as best we could.

We retired and consulted. Finally we laid before her a plan, suggested by the character of the matter itself, *viz.*, to make the work consist of four volumes, each divided into three parts: (1) the Stanzas and Commentaries thereon; (2) Symbolism; (3) Science. Further, instead of making the first volume to consist, as she had intended, of the history of some great Occultists, we advised her to follow the natural order of exposition, and begin with the Evolution of Cosmos, to pass from that to the Evolution of Man, then to deal with the historical part in a third volume treating of the lives of some great Occultists; and finally, to speak of Practical Occultism in a fourth volume should she ever be able to write it.

This plan we laid before H.P.B., and it was duly sanctioned by her.

The next step was to read the MSS. through again and make a general re-arrangement of the matter pertaining to the subjects coming under the heads of Cosmogony and Anthropology, which were to form the first two volumes of the work. When this had been completed, and H.P.B. duly consulted, and her approval of what had been done obtained, the whole of the MSS. so arranged was typewritten out by professional hands, then re-read, corrected, compared with the original MSS., and all Greek, Hebrew, and Sanskrit quotations inserted by us. It then appeared that the whole of the Commentary on the Stanzas did not amount to more than some twenty pages of the present work, as H.P.B. had not stuck closely to her text in writing. So we seriously interviewed her, and suggested that she should write a proper commentary, as in her opening words she had promised her readers to do. Her reply was characteristic: " What on earth am I to say? What *do* you want to know? Why it's all as plain as the nose on your face!!!" We could not see it; she didn't— or made out she didn't—so we retired to reflect.

As an interpolation, I had better state here that in the autumn of 1887—October, if I remember aright—we all moved into London, to 17, Lansdowne Road, Notting Hill, where the Countess Wachtmeister, who had been on a visit to Sweden ever since H.P.B. left Ostend, joined us in establishing the first T. S. Headquarters in London. During our stay at Maycot, *Lucifer* was founded, being published originally by Mr. G. Redway, H.P.B. keeping on all the while writing her articles, and also turning out further MSS. for *The Secret Doctrine*. These and other T.S.

work had to be attended to, and as sub-editor of *Lucifer* I found my hands pretty full, so that many weeks were consumed, and I think the removal to Lansdowne Road effected, before the problem of the Commentary on the Stanzas was finally solved.

The solution was this:—Each sloka of the stanzas was written (or cut out from the type-written copy) and pasted at the head of a sheet of paper, and then on a loose sheet pinned thereto were written all the questions we could find time to devise upon that sloka. In this task Mr. Richard Harte helped us very considerably, a large proportion of the questions put being of his devising. H.P.B. struck out large numbers of them, made us write fuller explanations, or our own ideas—such as they were—of what her readers expected her to say, wrote more herself, incorporated the little she had already written on that particular sloka, and so the work was done.

But when we came to think of sending the MSS. to the printers, the result was found to be such that the most experienced compositor would tear his hair in blank dismay. Therefore Dr. Keightley and myself set to work with a type-writer, and alternately dictating and writing, made a clean copy of the first parts of volumes I. and II.

Then work was continued till parts II. and III. of each volume were in a fairly advanced condition, and we could think of sending the work to press.

It had originally been arranged that Mr. George Redway should publish the work, but his proposals not being financially satisfactory, the needful money was offered by a friend of H.P.B.'s, and it was resolved to take the publication of *Lucifer* into our own hands. So the Duke Street office was taken, and business begun there, the primary object being to enable the T.S. to derive the utmost possible benefit from H.P.B.'s writings.

Of the further history of *The Secret Doctrine* there is not much more to say—though there were months of hard work before us. H.P.B. read and corrected two sets of galley proofs, then a page proof, and finally a revise in sheet, correcting, adding, and altering up to the very last moment:—result: printer's bill for corrections alone over £300.

Of phenomena in connection with *The Secret Doctrine*, I have very little indeed to say. Quotations with full references, from books which were never in the house—quotations verified after hours of search, sometimes, at the British Museum for a rare book—of such I saw and verified not a few.

In verifying them I found occasionally the curious fact that the numerical references were reversed, *e.g.*, p. 321 for p. 123, illustrating the reversal of objects when seen in the astral light. But beyond such instances of clairvoyant vision, I have no further phenomena directly bearing upon the production of *The Secret Doctrine* to record.

Finally I must not omit the valuable assistance which was rendered by Mr. E. D. Fawcett. Before I went to Ostend he had been in correspondence with H.P.B., and later on he also worked with and for her on the book at Lansdowne Road. He supplied many of the quotations from scientific works, as well as many confirmations of the occult doctrines derived from similar sources. It would not be right in giving any account of how *The Secret Doctrine* was written to omit to mention his name, and as I have not done so in the proper chronological sequence, I repair the omission now.

Of the value of the work, posterity must judge finally. Personally I can only place on record my profound conviction that when studied thoroughly but not treated as a revelation, when understood and assimilated but not made a text for dogma, H.P.B.'s *Secret Doctrine* will be found of incalculable value, and will furnish suggestions, clues, and threads of guidance, for the study of Nature and Man, such as no other existing work can supply.

B.K

II.

Dr. ARCHIBALD KEIGHTLEY'S

ACCOUNT OF THE

WRITING OF "THE SECRET DOCTRINE."

THE first news I had of *The Secret Doctrine* was the advertisement in *The Theosophist*. I was told in 1884 that Madame Blavatsky was engaged in writing a book, but I did not know what. Then I heard that the book was to be called *The Secret Doctrine*, that various people had been consulted as to its construction, and that all the moot points of Hindû Philosophy had been submitted to the late T. Subba Row, who had also made various suggestions as to its construction. Afterwards I found that he had done so, sketching out very roughly an outline, but this was not followed.

Then came the news that Madame Blavatsky's health had broken down and that she was compelled to leave India to save her life. I next heard of her as in Italy, at work, and finally at Würzburg, whence she came to Ostend.

Of the work done previous to my going to Ostend I know nothing. From various causes it came about that I went to Ostend to see H.P.B.; there I found her living with the Countess Wachtmeister, hard at work writing from six a.m. till six p.m., only omitting very short intervals for meals. She wrote and slept in one room, emerging to meals in the next room. When I arrived I learned that her susceptibility to cold was so great that the utmost care had to be used in airing her rooms during the winter.

Very soon after arriving I was handed a part of the MSS. with a request to emendate, excise, alter the English, punctuate, in fact treat it as my own, a privilege I naturally did not avail myself of. The MSS. was then in detached sections, similar to those included under the heads of " Symbolism " and "Appendices " in the published volumes. What I saw was a mass of MSS. with no definite arrangement, much of which had been patiently and industriously copied by the Countess Wachtmeister. The idea then was to keep one copy in Europe, while the other went to India for correction by various native collaborators. The greater part did go at a later date, but some cause prevented the collaboration.

What struck me most in the part I was able to read during my short stay was the enormous number of quotations from various authors. I knew that there was no library to consult and I could see that H.P.B.'s own books did not amount to thirty in all, of which several were dictionaries and several works counted two or more volumes. At this time I did not see the *Stanzas of Dzyan*, though there were several pieces of the *Occult Catechism* included in the MSS.

At a later date I again went to Ostend to carry out the arrangements for bringing H.P.B. to England. The main difficulty was to get her papers and books packed up. No sooner was one packed than it was wanted for reference; if part of the MSS. were put in a box it was certain to be that part which already contained some information which had to be cut out and placed elsewhere: and as H.P.B. continued to write until the very day before her departure, such was her unflagging industry, it was not an easy matter to get her belongings packed.

When she arrived at Norwood the reverse process went on, but the difficulty was to get unpacked quickly enough. One day was yielded, but six a.m. of the following day found her at her table. All through the summer of 1887 every day found her at work from six to six, with intervals for meals only, visitors being with very rare exceptions denied or told to come in the evening. The evenings were given up to talk and discussion, and only on rare occasions was any writing done then.

All through that summer Bertram Keightley and I were engaged in reading, re-reading, copying and correcting. The last amounted to casting some of the sentences in English mould, for many of them were " literal translations from the French." One remarkable fact is worth noticing. It was not long before the *genius loci* became apparent and in most of the MSS. written after the date of arrival in England there was very little of this kind of correction needed.

Many of the quotations had to be verified, and here we should have been lost if it had not been for a hint from H.P.B. She told us one night that sometimes in writing down quotations, which for the purpose of the book had been impressed on the Astral Light before her, she forgot to reverse the figures—for instance page 123 would be allowed to remain 321 and so on. With this in mind verification was easier, for one was puzzled on examining all editions in the British Museum to find in several cases that the books did not contain the number of pages. With the reversal matters were straightened out and the correct places found.

Much of the MSS. was type-written at this period. This was H.P.B.'s opportunity. The spaces were large and much could be inserted. Needless to say, it was. The thick type-MSS. were cut, pasted, recut and pasted several times over, until several of them were twice the size of the original MSS. But in it all was apparent that no work and no trouble, no suffering or pain could daunt her from her task. Crippled with rheumatism, suffering from a disease which had several times nearly proved fatal, she still worked on unflaggingly, writing at her desk the moment her eyes and fingers could guide the pen.

Then came the time of the founding of *Lucifer*. This work had to be added to that of writing *The Secret Doctrine*. As for the articles for Russian papers there were constant and imploring demands. None were to be had, for the pressure of other work was too great.

In September came the move to London, to Lansdowne Road. This was not so bad, for the books and papers could be arranged, packed and unpacked, and re-arranged the same day. The same method of work was followed and day succeeded day until the time came for going to press.

During the greater part of the period in London H.P.B. had the assistance of E. D. Fawcett, especially in those parts of the second volume dealing with the evolutionary hypotheses. He suggested, corrected, and wrote, and several pages of his MSS. were incorporated by H.P.B. into her work.

Needless to say our work went on. We had to carry the general scheme (if it would be called such in a work which was professedly a foe to the process of crystallization of thought) in our heads. We had to draw H.P.B.'s attention to the repetitions occurring in the isolated sections, and so far as possible in this way to act as watch-dogs and help her to make the meaning as clear as possible. But all the work was hers. A few stops here and there, a few suggestions, the correction of a French-spelled word, was ours; the rest was H.P.B.'s own, and all was approved by her.

During this period in London came inevitable interruptions; H.P.B. might try as she would, but friends and curiosity-seekers would not all be denied. Then, too, there was *Lucifer* with its regular monthly " Stand and Deliver " so much time and copy; Blavatsky Lodge and other meetings; letters to read and answer—all interfered with work. Failing health and strength came, and it was an increasing task to rise so early or to work so late. Still time continued and work went on, and the estimates of printers were examined. Certain requirements as to size of page and margin were particular points with H.P.B., as also were the thickness and quality of paper. Some of her critics had disliked the thickness of *Isis Unveiled*, so the paper had to be thinner so as to reduce the size. These points decided, the book began to go to press. It so happened that I was called into the country and so did not see the first half or more of the first volume as it passed. But it went through three or four other hands besides H.P.B.'s in galley proof, as well as in revise. She was her own most severe corrector, and was liable to treat revise as MSS., with alarming results in the correction item in the bill.

Then came the writing of the preface, and finally the book was out. The period of work and excitement was over and all was quiet till the first copy was delivered.

A. K.

III.

ABOUT "THE SECRET DOCTRINE"
By WILLIAM Q. JUDGE.

I HAVE been asked to write anything known to me personally about the writing of *The Secret Doctrine* by H. P. B. As but little time was then spent by me in the company of the author, what I have to say is meagre. If I had been with her as much when *The Secret Doctrine* was being put together as I was when she was writing *Isis*, very great benefit would have accrued to myself, and in view of a letter she wrote me from Würzburg, I have some regret that the opportunity offered was not availed of.

When the plan for *The Secret Doctrine* had taken definite shape in outline in her mind, H. P. B. wrote me several letters on the subject, one of which I will quote from:

"Würzburg, March 24th, 1886. Dear W. Q. J. I wish only you could spare two or three months and come to me at Ostende where I am emigrating again, to be nearer to — and friends. I have some money now and could easily pay your fare out and back. There's a dear, good fellow, *do* consent to it. You will be working for the Society, for I want you badly for the arrangement of *Secret Doctrine*. Such facts, *such facts*, Judge, as Masters are giving out will rejoice your old heart. Oh, how I *do* want you. The thing is becoming enormous, a wealth of facts. I need you for calculations and to write with me. I can assure you, you will not lose time by coming. . Do think of it, dear old boy. Yours sincerely and affectionately, H. P. B."

This pressing invitation I could not accept because of certain circumstances, but on looking back at it I am sorry that it was let slip by. Other letters going into the matter of what was to be done and referring to old beginnings need not be quoted. One of them, however, reminds me of another period when *The Secret Doctrine* was in her mind, though I am not aware she had told anyone else. It was in Paris in 1884, where I had gone to meet her. We stopped in a house in the Rue Notre Dame des Champs, and for a shorter time at the country house of the Count and Countess d'Adhémar at Enghien near Paris. At Enghien especially, H. P. B. wanted me to go carefully through the pages of her copy of *Isis Unveiled* for the purpose of noting on the margins what subjects were treated, and for the work she furnished me with what she called a special blue and red pencil. I went all through both volumes and made the notes required, and of those she afterwards wrote me that they were of the greatest use to her. During our stay there several psychical phenomena took place seen by many persons. But every night while others were asleep I was often awake for several hours, and then in the quiet and the darkness saw and heard many things which no one else but H. P. B. knew of. Among these were hundreds of astral signal bells flying back and forth, showing—to those who know the meaning under such things—that much was on foot when people were asleep and the place free from disturbances of noise and ill-feeling common to the waking mortal.

At the house in Paris she worked all day and often far into the night on the book, and conversed with me about it. Sometimes she became changed in manner and much absorbed, so much so that automatically the famous cigarettes were lighted and then forgotten. In that way one night she lighted and let go out so many that I forgot to keep count.

One day I said to her that I would write the book entire, for a joke. She took me up seriously, saying that I might and she would see that I accomplished it, but I declined of course. This was in private, and there was no attempt at guying at all. The subject of elementals came up, and I asked her if she intended to give much on it. Her reply was that she might say something, but it was all *sub judice* as yet and must wait for orders, as it was not a quiet or harmless part of the thing.

She then asked me to write down all I knew or thought I knew on that head, and she would see if that much coming from me would be allowed to pass the unseen critics. A long chapter on Elementals was then done, nearly all by my pen, and she put it away for some time. The day that it was finished was warm and pleasant, and in the middle of the afternoon she suddenly grew absorbed once more. The air of the room at the same time was turned to the temperature of much below freezing, to judge by sensation, and I remarked on the fact. It was not a change of the weather at all, but seemed to blow out from H. P. B. as if she was an open door from some huge refrigerating store. I again drew her attention to it and said, "It feels as if a door was open on the Himalaya Mountains and the cold air was blowing into this room."

To this she replied: "Perhaps it is so," and smiled. It was so cold that I had to protect myself with a rug taken from the floor.

In about three days she announced that my small and inadequate chapter on Elementals had been of such a sort that it was decided she would not put much, if anything, into *The Secret Doctrine* on the subject, and mine was either destroyed or retained. It certainly is not in any part of the published volumes.

Speaking to those who know and believe that H. P. B. was all the time in communication with the Masters in their retreats somewhere on the globe, I can say that a serious series of consultations was held among them as to what should go into *The Secret Doctrine*, and that it was plainly said that the book was to be done in such a manner as to compel the earnest student to dig out many profound truths which in a modern book would be announced especially and put down in regular course. It was also said from the same source that this age, being a transition one in all respects, the full revelations were not for this generation. But enough was to be given out in the manner described, as well as plainly, to make it substantially a revelation. All students, then, who are in earnest will do well not to pass carelessly over the pages of any part of the book.

This is all I can say on the subject of the writing of this wonderful book. I only wish it were more, and can but blame myself that I was not present at a time when, as I know now, greater opportunity was offered than at any other period for inner knowledge of the writers, seen and nseen, of *The Secret Doctrine*.

WILLIAM Q. JUDGE.

IV.

A FREE TRANSLATION

FROM THE ARTICLE IN THE

"RUSSIAN REVIEW" OF MOSCOW

ON

HELENA PETROVNA BLAVATSKY,

BY HER SISTER,

MADAME DE JELIHOWSKY.

IN the summer of 1886 I again visited my sister in Germany, where she was staying in Elberfeld, with her friends the Gebhards. As usual she was always surrounded by lots of people, some of whom came with the special aim of making her acquaintance and others to renew old friendships; but in Elberfeld, it seemed to me, she had more friends with kindly feelings towards her personality than drawn to her through her teachings.

At the beginning of our stay there Helena Petrovna was not able to work, but as soon as she was better all our time was spent in very interesting, lively conversations on the terrace or in the garden, and sometimes in reading the materials for *The Secret Doctrine* she was then writing. During these readings two characteristic points struck me especially, *viz.*, the wonderful picturesqueness of language and detailed descriptions when Helena Petrovna spoke, giving explanations on all kinds of questions asked her by specialists, and at the same time her perfect inability to keep to a purely scientific presentation of the evidences and the formulas.

Her talk was always entrancing, but as soon as she came to mathematical data, it constantly occurred that she was not able to read the algebraical and geometrical conclusions written down by her personality. Very often when left alone with her, I expressed my astonishment to her :—

"How can it be, that you, having calculated and written all this down yourself, can't read it?"

To this question my sister always replied, with hearty laughter,

"Do you expect me to know the problems of the higher mathematics? Your daughters are *bas bleus* and have learnt all these erudite matters, but, as to you and myself, have not we learned side by side, and did not we have the greatest trouble to master the first four rules of arithmetic?"

"Then how is it that you have written all this without knowing anything about it?"

"Come, now, don't be so *naïve!* As if you don't know there are many things in my writings of which I never dreamed before. *I* do not write them, I only copy out what is ready made before my eyes. I know that you always disbelieved me, but in this you see one more proof that I am only the tool and not the master."

"This does not prevent your descriptions from being masterly. It sounds as if you saw all this personally, and have visited all the places you speak about."

"I am not so sure about visiting, but as to seeing—of course I saw them, and I see constantly everything that I describe."

Such were her usual and constant answers.

V

A NOTE

FROM

MADAME VERA JOHNSTONE,

NIECE OF H.P.B.

DEAR COUNTESS WACHTMEISTER,

In June, 1886, I stayed with my aunt in Elberfeld and then in Ostend. It was her habit to read out in the afternoon what was written of *The Secret Doctrine* in the preceding night. Not knowing much English then I am sorry to say I was seldom present at these readings and only half understood the conversations that ensued, so that my contribution to your interesting book must be very small.

Generally on coming down in the morning from the bedroom I occupied in the house of Madame Gebhard together with my mother, I found my aunt deep in her work. So far as I know, she never wrote at that time in the morning, but carefully went over what was written the previous night. One day I saw evident traces of perplexity written on her face. Not wishing to disturb her I sat down quietly and waited for her to speak. She remained silent a long time with her eyes fixed on some point on the wall, and with a cigarette between her fingers, as was her custom. At last she called out to me:

"Vera," she said, "do you think you could tell me what is a pi?"

Rather astonished at such a question, I said I thought a pie was some kind of an English dish.

"Please don't make a fool of yourself," she said rather impatiently, "don't you understand I address you in your capacity of a mathematical pundit. Come and see this."

I looked at the page that lay before her on the table, and saw it was covered with figures and calculations, and soon became aware that the formula $\Pi = 3\cdot 14159$ was put down wrongly throughout them all. It was written $\Pi = 31\cdot 4159$. With great joy and triumph I hastened to inform her of her mistake.

"That's it!" she exclaimed. "This confounded comma bothered me all the morning. I was rather in a hurry yesterday to put down what I saw, and to-day at the first glance at the page I intensely but vaguely felt there was something wrong, and do what I could I could not remember where the comma actually was when I saw this number."

Knowing very little of Theosophy in general and my aunt's ways of writing in particular at that time, I of course was greatly struck with her not being able to correct such a slight mistake in the very intricate calculations she had written down with her own hand.

"You are very green," she said, "if you think that I actually know and understand all the things I write. How many times am I to repeat to you and your mother that the things I write are dictated to me, that sometimes I see manuscripts, numbers, and words before my eyes of which never knew anything."

On reading *The Secret Doctrine* several years later I

recognised the page. It was one of the pages which discuss Hindu astronomy. Later on, when we three went to Ostend, it was I who put aunt's things and books in order, so I can testify that the first month or two in Ostend she decidedly had no other books but a few French novels, bought at railway stations and read whilst travelling, and several odd numbers of some Russian newspapers and magazines. So that there was absolutely nothing where her numerous quotations could have come from.

Yours very sincerely,
VERA JOHNSTONE

P.S.—I append a letter received by me from Dr. Franz Hartmann:—

HALLEIN,
June 2nd, 1893.

MY DEAR MRS. JOHNSTONE,

With regard to our conversation referring to the way in which *The Secret Doctrine* was written, I beg to say that in April, 1885, when I accompanied H. P. Blavatsky from Madras to Europe, while on board of the S.S. "Tibre" and on the open sea, she very frequently received in some occult manner many pages of manuscript referring to *The Secret Doctrine*, the material of which she was collecting at that time. Miss Mary Flynn was with us, and knows more about it than I; because I did not take much interest in those matters, as the receiving of "occult correspondence" had become almost an everyday occurrence with us.

Yours very truly,
F. HARTMANN.

VI.

EXTRACTS

FROM A LETTER RECEIVED BY

The COUNTESS WACHTMEISTER From Dr. HÜBBE-SCHLEIDEN,

Editor of the "Sphinx".

Before I made H.P.B.'s personal acquaintance I received the letter from one of the Masters "*viâ* H.S.O." about which a good deal has been written, both in reports of the S.P.R. and elsewhere. The principal parts of this letter have also been repeatedly printed, thus I need not go back to it here. But I will say in regard to the S.P.R. report, that I do not care in the least whether that letter was written in Tibet or in London, by H.P.B. herself automatically, or even consciously inspired. Anyone who knows something of spiritual matters will never judge the value of such a letter from the *way* it is conveyed to him, or even how and where it is put on paper, but from its *contents* and from the power it has and exercises. In the same way I do *not* estimate the value of H.P.B. from the phenomena she produced (and I saw many of them) but from her teachings, and these I consider to be of the greatest importance, almost inestimable.

Four or five times I have spent periods of different lengths with her. The first time from September to

December, 1884 (about three months) when she stayed with the Gebhards in Elberfeld, where I had before met her for a few days in August of the same year. After that I remained with her in Würzburg about a week or ten days in October, 1885, and I saw her last, one afternoon and night, early in January, 1886. Thus I had many opportunities to learn a good deal from her and about her, all the more so as she was always exceedingly kind to me and very seldom grew tired of my many questions.

I saw almost all the phenomena that she did at the Gebhard's, most of which have often been told and printed. One of them, however, I believe is but little known.

Mr. Schmiechen had made duplicate copies of those two Mahâtmâ portraits which were afterwards sent to Adyar. These duplicates were given to Madame Mary Gebhard. The copies were so much like the originals that it was often disputed which were which. Only H.P.B., Olcott, and Mr. Schmiechen were never in doubt; and in order to stop these doubts one evening H.P.B. said: "Just wait, now leave those pictures alone!" at the same time evidently concentrating all her powers on them. Not many seconds afterwards she said: "Now turn them round." We did so, and found on the back of each portrait the well-known corresponding signatures of the Masters, one in blue, the other in red. But there would be no end were I to speak of all the phenomena. I will only add that I heard her produce the "knocks" and the "astral bells," still in the Autumn of 1885 at Würzburg. Once she felt too weak to do it alone; she required the assistance of one of the ladies present as her "medium," to supply astral force. I believe it was Mrs. Schmiechen then who willingly served her as one. Then we heard the knocks, as many as we wished and wherever we wished; in the table, on the looking-glass, in the cupboard, etc.

Several times I noticed that she could evidently read other people's thoughts; whether she could do so always I do not know. I should think that would depend on the power of that mind which she had to read, or perhaps on its spirituality.

Now for the main thing. What I know about *The Secret Doctrine.*

When I visited her in October, 1885, she had just begun to write it, and in January, 1886, she had finished about a dozen chapters. While I occupied myself chiefly with Babaji, who was then living with her, she was writing at her manuscript almost all day, from the early morning until the afternoon and even until night, unless she had guests. At that time she wrote articles for *The Theosophist* as well.* But she had scarcely any books, not half a dozen, and I had to procure for her an English Bible, either to quote some text correctly or to control the correctness of some quotation.

In many respects her work was then carried on in a very similar way to that which Col. Olcott describes in Chapter xiii. of his "Old Diary Leaves," in the April number of *The Theosophist.* I also saw her write down sentences as if she were copying them from something before her, where, however, I saw nothing. I did not pay much attention to the manner of her work from the standpoint of a hunter of phenomena, and did not control it for that purpose; but I know that I saw a good deal of the well-known blue K.H. handwriting as corrections and annotations on her manuscripts as well as in books that lay occasionally on

* For instance: "Have animals souls?"

her desk. And I noticed this principally in the morning before she had commenced to work. I slept on the couch in her study after she had withdrawn for the night, and the couch stood only a few feet from her desk. I remember well my astonishment one morning when I got up to find a great many pages of foolscap covered with that blue pencil handwriting lying on her own manuscript, at her place on her desk. How these pages got there I do not know, but I did not see them before I went to sleep and no person had been bodily in the room during the night, for I am a light sleeper.

I must say though that the view I took then was the same that I hold now. I never did and never shall judge of the value or the origin of any mental product from the way and manner in which it is produced. And for this reason I withheld my opinion then, thinking and saying: " I shall wait until *The Secret Doctrine* is finished and then I can read it quietly; that will be the test for me, the only one that will be any good."

This is the reason *why* on the night of my last parting from H.P.B., the two *certificates*, which were printed for the first time in the last April number of *The Path*, page 2, were given to me. At least I found them in my copy of Hodgson's S.P.R. Report after I had left her. *I* am the person who showed them to Mr. Judge in London last August. From the advice given me in the one signed K.H. I was not to publish them, but Mr. Judge was authorised to do so by the instructions which *he* received.

In concluding I will repeat that I consider *The Secret Doctrine* of H.P.B. to be a book of the utmost importance, for I have not the least doubt that it really *does* contain the *Secret Doctrine*, the sacred wisdom of all sages and of all

H

ages. In it are given the only true and useful (expedient) keys which can solve the riddles of existence as well of the *macrocosm* as of the *microcosm*. I find it, however, very desirable, if not necessary, that explanatory abstracts should be written to it, in order to turn the contents to better use for *present* readers. That is the reason that I wrote my abstract from it in 1891, which I called *Lust, Leid und Liebe*, which confined itself to the language and to the terms of Darwin, Haeckel and modern philosophy, with the purpose of putting a key to *The Secret Doctrine* into the hands of the leading scientists. My effort found no grace with the English public, but some in Germany.

Finally, I think it is an absolutely useless question, *who* wrote H.P.B.'s *Secret Doctrine*. It was written with her pen: but whether *she* was the adept herself, or some other adept or adepts wrote it through her and with her, is quite immaterial for the work itself and its indisputable value.

FROM *THE PATH*, APRIL, 1893, p. 2.

THE first certificate alluded to in the preceding paragraphs runs thus :—

" I wonder if this note of mine is worthy of occupying a select spot with the documents reproduced, and which of the peculiarities of the 'Blavatskian' style of writing it will be found to most resemble? The present is simply to satisfy the doctor that 'the more proof given the less believed.' Let him take my advice and not make these two documents public. It is for his own satisfaction the undersigned is happy to assure him that *The Secret Doctrine*, when ready, will be the triple production of [here are the names of one of the Masters and of H.P.B.] and —— most humble servant," [signed by the other].

On the back of this was the following, signed by the Master who is mentioned in the above:—

"If this can be of any use or help to——, though I doubt it, I, the humble undersigned Faquir, certify that *The Secret Doctrine* is dictated to [name of H.P.B.] partly by myself and partly by my brother ——."

A year after this, certain doubts having arisen in the minds of individuals, another letter from one of the signers of the foregoing was sent, and read as follows. As the prophecy in it has come true, it is now the time to publish it for the benefit of those who know something of how to take and understand such letters. For the outside it will all be so much nonsense:

" The certificate given last year, saying that *The Secret Doctrine* would be, when finished, the triple production of [H.P.B.'s name], ——, and myself, was and is correct, although some have doubted not only the facts given in it, but also the authenticity of the message in which it was contained. Copy this, and also keep the copy of the aforesaid certificate. You will find them both of use on the day when you shall, as will happen without your asking, receive from the hands of the very person to whom the certificate was given, the original for the purpose of allowing you to copy it; and then you can verify the correctness of this presently forwarded copy. And it may then be well to indicate to those wishing to know what portions in *The Secret Doctrine* have been copied by the pen of [H.P.B.'-

name] into its pages, though without quotation marks, from my own manuscript and perhaps from ——, though the last is more difficult from the rarity of his known writing and greater ignorance of his style. All this and more will be found necessary as time goes on, but for which you are well qualified to wait."

VII.
EVIDENCE FROM A MODERN SCIENTIST.

DR. CARTER BLAKE, to whom we are indebted for the following remarks, was in 1863 one of the secretaries of Section E (British Association for the Advancement of Science). He was born in London in 1840, and has pursued the study of zoölogy from an early age. His connection with the periodical literature of the scientific world has existed for many years. He was early connected with Her Majesty's Civil Service in the War Office of London and, during the period which succeeded the invasion of Morocco by the Spanish forces in 1859, and the negotiations which were on foot to procure the ransom agreed on for the capture of Tetuan, was secretary to the Moorish Envoys in England. For a long time he was a pupil of and assistant to Professor, afterwards Sir Richard Owen, under whom his geological and palæontological studies were carried on. In 1862 he delivered to the London Institution a series of lectures on the Elementary Principles of Zoölogy. In the same year he was appointed to aid the celebrated Dr. Robert Knox in the classification of the Museum of the now defunct Ethnological Society of London. He is the author of many detached papers in scientific works and periodicals, *Modern Thought, Medico-chirurgical Review, Edinburgh Review, Morning Chronicle, Pall Mall Gazette, Reader, Parthenon, Geological Magazine, Medical Times, Geologist, Food Journal, Annals of Natural History, Anthropological Review, Transactions of Philological Society, Brande's Dictionary of Science, Literature, and Art, Alpine Guide*, and others, as well as the editor of *Knox's Manual of Zoölogy*, a second edition of which has been recently published. He was one of the original members of the Anthropological Society of London, of which he was honorary secretary at its establishment, and now lives to see it a successful and prosperous institution. In 1866 he was during a lengthened period investigating the geological features of the districts of south-eastern Belgium. He is the editor of Broca's important work on *Hybridity in the Genus Homo*. In 1867 he gave up his official connection with the Anthropological Society, and resided in Nicaragua for nearly a year, where he had opportunities for studying the life and languages of the Indian aborigines in their own homes, and on his return visited New York. He was from 1868 to 1881 Lecturer on Comparative Anatomy at Westminster Hospital, and in 1871 reconstructed the Museum of the Hull Literary and Philosophical Society according to modern scientific principles. In 1875 he published a work, *Zoölogy for Students*, to which a preface was written by Professor Owen. In 1881 he was translator of *Fau's Artistic Anatomy*, in 1883 author of a *Guide to the Fisheries Exhibition*, in 1884 *Guide to the Health Exhibition*, and a translation of Rochet's work on *The Natural Proportions of Both Sexes*, and in 1885 a translation of Dusart's work on *Phosphate of Lime*. Many translations of Spanish, French, Latin and German works are from his pen; and he has several times lectured in the Natural History Department of the British Museum, under the auspices of Sir Richard Owen. His attainments and his close connection with H.P.B. give value to his opinion on the points with which he deals, and special interest to the following communication.—(ED.)

On ordinary lines it is strange that an old, sickly woman,

not consulting a library and having no books of her own of consequence, should possess the unusual knowledge that Madame Blavatsky undoubtedly did. Indeed, it is incomprehensible, unless she were of an extraordinary mental capacity, and had spent her whole life in study. On the contrary, from many sources we gain undoubted evidence that Madame Blavatsky's education had not even been carried as far as that of a High School student of the present day.

But it is a fact that she knew more than I did on my own particular lines of anthropology, etc. For instance, her information was superior to my own on the subject of the Naulette Jaw. Page 744 in the second vol. of *The Secret Doctrine* refers to facts which she could not easily have gathered from any published book.

On page 754, also of the second vol. *Secret Doctrine*, the sentence beginning: "If we turn to the new world," and speaking of the existence of "pliocene mammalia and the occurrence of pliocene raised beaches." I remember in conversation with her in 1888, in Lansdowne Road, at the time she was engaged on *The Secret Doctrine*, how Madame Blavatsky, to my great astonishment, sprung upon me the fact that the raised beaches of Tarija were pliocene. I had always thought them pleistocene—following the line of reasoning of Darwin and Spotswood Wilson.

The fact that these beaches are pliocene has been proven to me since from the works of Gay, *Istoria Fiscia de Chile*, Castlenaw's book on Chile, and other works, though these out-of-the-way books had never then come into my hands, in spite of the fact that I had made a *spécialité* of the subject; and not until Madame Blavatsky put me on the track of the pliocene did I hear of them.

On page 755, II. *Secret Doctrine*, her mention of the fossil footprints from Carson, Indiana, U.S.A., is again interesting as a proof that she did not obtain her information by thought-reading. When Madame Blavatsky spoke of the footprints to me I did not know of their existence, and Mr. G. W. Bloxam, Assistant Secretary of the Anthropological Institute, afterwards told me that a pamphlet on the subject in their library had never been out.

Madame Blavatsky certainly had original sources of information (I don't say what) transcending the knowledge of experts on their own lines.

C. CARTER BLAKE.

28, Townshend Road, N.W.
January 27th, 1893.

VIII.

A PRIVATE LETTER.

Dear Countess Wachtmeister,

As you are preparing a book upon H.P.B.'s method of writing *The Secret Doctrine*, you may like to include a sketch of her method of personally teaching her pupils at a distance.

Nothing has heretofore been printed upon this subject, nor could I do so if my name were appended to the account. Yet I think you and others will accept my statements especially as some of you have had proof that I was so taught, as, I doubt not, were others, though I do not know of them.

It is because this method in part resembles her description of how she was taught herself, and how she wrote *Isis* and *The Secret Doctrine*, that I think it will be interesting in this connection.

Living some thousand of miles from England, I never met Madame Blavatsky in person. It is now seven years since first I heard her name, and the word "Theosophy." Like others of my acquaintance, I first heard of both by coming across the S.P.R. pamphlet denouncing her as an impostor and asserting the Hodgson-Coulomb slander as a true fact. Against this weak background with its feeble personalities, her colossal individuality stood sharply outlined, astonishing the spectators of this shallow age. It is not my habit to judge of persons by any specific acts, but by the whole tendency of their teaching or their lives. H.P.B. herself wrote at about that time:—

" Follow the path I show, the Masters who are behind : do not follow me or my path."

I first took this as pointing out in herself, that common human liability to fail in living the truths it teaches and would fain attain, and I was willing to extend to Madame Blavatsky, the courageous Messenger, that lenient judgment which we ourselves ask for in like case.

Soon, however, I began to realise, through my own experience, that she was not what she seemed to be. Upon this point I will not dwell, further than to say that the evidence I had, caused me to ask H.P.B. to teach me; and the fact that I fully trusted in and believed her, is precisely what gained for me the fulfilment of my wish. The mental attitude of belief sets up, in our aura and in our inner bodies, magnetic and attractive conditions, very different to those of contraction and densification, which exist where doubt or criticism fill the mind. A literal quickening of my aura and inner body took place; the former was felt even by persons to whom my thoughts and Theosophic interests were all unknown. The contraction in which men and women enfold themselves is too little understood. To be known, faith and devotion must first be had. I have heard tell of one of her readers who said that Madame Blavatsky never published anything about the human aura. What a ripple of amusement then went the rounds of those who have any clues to *The Secret Doctrine* or knowledge of certain other matters !

The situation was then this. I was at a great distance from H.P.B. Madame Blavatsky died before I ever met her. I was not, I never became a " Psychic " as that word is generally used. I had no wish for "powers," never sat for "meditation" or "concentration." It is, however, natural for me to concentrate upon whatever I do, and Theosophy is never out of my mind. I was not and I am not a vegetarian. I had taken no ascetic vows. I had never had any "psychic," clairvoyant or subjective experiences (except those of thought) in my life. I lived quite another life until Theosophy expanded my mind and urged me to strenuous efforts in study and T.S. work, in order that help might come to all those minds obscured by the chill sense of being alone and helpless in a world of chance, where no internal peace could be gained save through the narcotization of Dogma, Doctrine or Convention. The use of narcotics—even for the mind—becomes in time a new form of suffering.

After H.P.B. accepted me as a pupil, no rules were laid down, no plans formulated. I continued my daily routine, and at night, after I fell into a deep sleep, the new life began. On waking in the morning from a sleep so profound that the attitude of the previous night was still retained, I would vividly remember that I had gone, as it were, to H.P.B. I had been received in rooms which I could and did describe to those who lived with her—described, even to the worn places or holes in the carpet. On the first occasion of this kind she signified to me her acceptance of me as a pupil and in no other way. After that, she would receive me in varying fashion, showing me pictures which passed like panoramas across the walls of the room.

There are but few that I could verbally describe, containing as they do methods of Motion, of vibration, of the formation of a world from the first nucleolus, of "Spirit moulding matter" into form, of Motion that was Consciousness and that was precipitated in my brain as a picture of a fact or a truth. There were definite things too, facts given in *The Secret Doctrine* and in other teachings, none of these being published at the time. Many more things than I can name were thus taught to me, such as future events, events then actually occurring, and facts still unknown relative to the lives of other persons or of the T.S. At other times, times more rare, I would awake to find her standing at the foot of my bed, and as I leaned upon my elbow, her sign-language would begin, the harmonies of Nature would fill the moonlit room, while the wondrous living pictures passed across the wall. All this was perfectly objective to me. I was fully awake to all the surroundings, to all the natural sounds of the night, and I have taken my pet dog into my arms because it shivered and whimpered at sight of her. All the expressions of H.P.B.'s face became familiar to me. I can see her now, her old bedgown—what dingy old gown was ever so cherished?—folded about her, as she opened out space before me, and then, too, expanded into her own real being.

I have hardly more than half-a-dozen letters from her, and these contain no teaching; they bore upon external theosophic affairs and have this peculiarity. At night she would tell me to advise certain persons of certain things. I would obey, giving her as my authority, and a few days afterwards, but never long enough for the full voyage, would come her letter giving in writing the instructions previously heard at night. Thus I was enabled to prove that I really heard her wish over seas, for always the request concerned some sudden emergency which had just arisen a day, two days at most, before. I was able to check off my experience in this way, as I was also able to speak at times before an event occurred. I never went into a trance but once, and that was after Madame Blavatsky's death. I never had anything to do with spiritualism or mediums. After a short time, I was able to see and to hear at will, without training or effort, as simply and as easily as one breathes. I could see a distant place or person or hear a reply to a question at will. I never made a mistake, though those who had the right, tested me. But let me hasten to add also that I never did any of these things for idle curiosity, but only for the work of Theosophy, and that such use of force at will is with me comparatively infrequent. I do not know how far it extends, simply because I do not care to know.

There are persons who hope to turn us to the belief that H. P. B. was no more than a chela, deserted at the last. But to this day the things she foretold keep on coming true, aye, even to their tempting us, even to definite events for which she prepared us by forewarning us. So all the clatter and chatter, the turmoil and revelations leave us undisturbed, and the apostles of a revised teaching reveal their ignorance of what she taught as clues, clues which they cannot find. The proof, the ever-recurring, ever-living proof, is ours.

There were thus two classes of events. First, those in which she taught me, or in which persons, to me objective, would appear and would show me certain things, or when voices would speak bringing news which came again later on, by post or otherwise. The second class was made up of those minor occasions in which I used my own will.

Well do I remember that night when H. P. B. commanded me to use the developing powers for the Theosophical Society only, and to beware of the psychic will-o'-the-wisp.

What I write may seem vague. I will give instances. I was about to enter upon a plan of work with a person whom I was meeting for the first time. All at once I saw in the air H.P.B.'s beautiful hand—the hand with the seal ring upon it—drawing along the atmosphere, just at the height of my eyes, a series of pictures. These pictures represented a course of events and caused me to change my plans; some time after I verified the occurrences. Once I was forewarned of a death which took place at some distance, at the very hour of the warning. Again, I trusted and leaned much upon a certain person, who was gaining an influence over my mind as one learned in spiritual things. One night H.P.B. came, leading this person by the hand, and drawing the skin away from the body of her companion, showed me the internal organs in a hideous state of disease. H.P.B. then pointed to the corner of the room; a bright star seemed to shoot from the heavens and to fall into an abyss. H.P.B. made a sign (and her language was one of signs which vibrated through the ether and seemed to fall into my brain as thoughts), the sign and gesture meant :—" Trust not the fallen star." All this came true, horribly, sadly true.

These events continue to take place, but I must note a difference in their method of occurrence since the death of Madame Blavatsky.

1. I do not see that person.
2. The events occur almost always in the daytime.
3. I am almost always fully conscious on the objective material plane as well.

4. The exceptions to 3 are when my consciousness seems to function in another time or place or body, but even then they occupy but a few seconds apparently, inasmuch as the people about me will have noticed nothing, and I have apparently continued my previous occupation, while I have, so far as my own consciousness goes, been living quite a time in other ages, planes or places. For instance, while dressing in the morning and thinking of the day's plans, I have at the same time felt myself to be in the body of a friend who was then in a steamer in mid-ocean, fastening his collar-button before a mirror, cursing it because it would not fasten, and thinking of me. His sea-trunk lay open behind him. I took a note of the day and hour and subsequently verified his action. The curious part of it is that I felt myself to be both persons and continued both trains of thought at one and the same time.

5. I use my will much more frequently than I did.

And finally, this. A few days after Madame Blavatsky died, H. P. B. awoke me at night. I raised myself, feeling no surprise, but only the sweet accustomed pleasure. She held my eyes with her leonine gaze. Then she grew thinner, taller, her shape became masculine; slowly then her features changed, until a man of height and rugged powers stood before me, the last vestige of her features melting into his, until the leonine gaze, the progressed radiance of her glance alone remained. The man lifted his head and said: "Bear witness!" He then walked from the room, laying his hand on the portrait of H. P. B. as he passed. Since then he has come to me several times, with instructions, in broad daylight while I was busily working, and once he stepped out from a large portrait of H. P. B

In closing this partial sketch of an inner life which goes on *pari passu* with the outer, let me impress upon you the fact that I never seek or look for any of these things, just as I never use my will to see or hear except when impelled from within. H. P. B. taught me to be "positive" on the psychic plane and "receptive" to higher planes or Beings alone. She taught that the mind was all. Whatever development I gained, came unsought, I never made myself "passive." I am, when awake, at all times able to use whatever gifts I have; I found them within myself and I use them instinctively, naturally, although I had no trace of them before I found H.P.B. Rarely, very rarely now, do I get things in dreams.

It is my firm conviction, based upon experience, that to the sole fact of my devotion to the Lodge, the T.S. and H.P.B., do I owe any of these teachings. This devotion no shock can impair, for my double life and all my consciousness daily prove what these high truths are. In that belief and in the hope that my experience may quicken the seeds of devotion in other minds, I give this out impersonally, for H.P.B. showed me that the mind was all, and how she came to break the moulds of human minds and to set them free. The real H.P.B. was disclosed, and I am one of those who have no difficulty in reconciling all the facts of her outer existence, for some there are who can see behind the veils used by the high occultist when dealing with the unseen at the heart of material things.

Thus taught, in the harmonious nights, that H.P.B. who wrote:—

"My days are my Pralayas, my nights are my Manvantaras."

Blessed, indeed, are those who shared her Manvantaras, and who " have not seen and yet have believed."

R. S.

NOTE.—It has been suggested to me that this rapid unfolding without ascetic practice, was due to my "getting back" what was before known to me. I cannot say yea or nay to this, for I know nothing about it. What appears to be necessary, in occultism, is that *each should follow the doctrine of his own Teacher with regard to himself.* There are many souls at various stages of evolution, each with its own requirements. Moreover, the requirements of practical occultism, the evolution of force in one's self, are again different. To these I have not been attracted, in this life at least. But above all, Devotion to the ideal of the Teachers and to the work, is the firm ground upon which to stand.

R. S

APPENDIX II.

EXTRACTS

FROM ARTICLES, INTERVIEWS, ETC., THAT HAVE APPEARED IN

THE PUBLIC PRESS.

FROM *THE PATH*, AUGUST, 1888.

THE THEOSOPHICAL SOCIETY AND MADAME BLAVATSKY.

THE following letter has been received from a valuable contributor, and we deem it of sufficient importance to print it in this place:—

DEAR BROTHER JUDGE,

With pleasure I acknowledge the receipt of your letter, asking whether I am prepared to support H. P. Blavatsky in whatever course she may pursue.

While I know that the action of an individual matters but little, I know also that it does have its due effect; a loyal heart is one of the occult powers. Hence I am very glad to answer that I do and shall at all times, in all places and to all persons *unqualifiedly* sustain Madame Blavatsky. I will follow her lead so long as I understand her, and when I cannot understand I will follow with my intuition; when that fails I will blindly and doggedly follow still.

For this course there are reasons. Intuition and analogy alike furnish them. They lie at the very basis of the unseen or occult world, and that world is the only real one. It is not a world of form like ours. Here all tends to form, to segregation, to crystallization ; consequently to limitations and boundaries. This is true alike of forms social and political, religious, civic, and domestic ; it is also true of the minds of men ; they also, against our best interest and endeavour, strive to cast us in a mould, that the free soul may not do its boundless work in us, and in order to bind us yet awhile to Nature and the lower natural order.

In that other world which is the true, this order changes. This world is subversive of forms. Its influence penetrates so far into the material world in this respect, that its subversion becomes the condition of free growth. The life condition is one of sloughing off as well as receiving, and all nervous action proceeds by ganglionic shocks.

So it must be with the Theosophical Society if i is to live and expand in helpfulness and power. Men must fall away from us even as the forest sheds the autumnal leaf. Shocks must occur, not alone coming from the outside, but internal shocks, the necessary efforts of the Theosophical organism to adjust itself to the laws of growth.

Many there be who lament these effects ; it is because they know them not as laws. I am as enamoured of peace as any man, but I do not choose it at the expense of spiritual growth. For us there is no real and lasting peace outside of Eternity. This is a dark age ; there is stern work to be done. The lurid action of this cycle is not to be turned by repose, by "sweetness and light."

Let all weak and wounded souls fall to the rear—and let us get to that work. There is none too much time to do it in. *The future of the race is now at stake.* It is seed time and the ground must be harrowed and torn. I know that there is one who has devoted all her being to this work; one who under beneficent and all-wise suggestions is hastening it on; concentrating Karma and bringing it to a head in all directions; culminating these internal shocks that the organism may grow faster, that it may be able to stand alone forcefully when it has lost her, and that by its increased usefulness it may merit and obtain increase of spiritual influence, a new out-pour of power and aid from that unseen world where Karma is the sole arbiter. And any man or woman may know this as absolutely as you and I and some others do, who will take the trouble to consider the matter from the standpoint of soul and not from that of mind alone.

Then, too, there is the standpoint of heart, and it is of great value. What says the Ramâyana? " Be grateful. Sages prescribe expiations for murderers, robbers, drunkards, and other sinners, but no expiation can wash away the sin of one whose *offence is ingratitude*." Why is this? All these sayings are based upon universal laws. So I can tell you (and you know it) why this offence is so deep; why this " sin " cannot be pardoned. It is because " Karma is inflexibly just, and he who breaks a chain of influence by refusing to recognise the source whence it comes to him, and by turning aside from that source, has by his own act perverted the stream from his door. His punishment is simply this; the stream fails him; he discovers in aftertimes the full and arid misery of his position." In our world here below we think we stand as isolated centres of energy, having no vital connection with one another and the world at large except by our own will. We do indeed succeed in locking up a tremendous amount of forceful energy by thus impeding its free flow But as the evolutionary order and the very nature of Deity are against us, sooner or later we are swept aside, but not without repeated opportunities of choice. These occasions are now repeatedly furnished us in matters Theosophical by H. P. Blavatsky; in every test surmounted, in every glimpse of intuition or act of faith we grow. We do not grow as a body or as individuals when, from lack of these virtues and from being ungrateful, we fail to give in our constant adhesion to her who stands in this dark age as the Messenger of the Higher Powers. For in that other world, through and with which she works, there are hierarchies held inviolable from cycle to cycle: vast organizations formed by universal law wherein every member stands in his own order and merit, and can no more be expunged or disregarded by those above or below him than I can blot out a star. All efface themselves for this work, re-incarnating again and again for it alone. There is no other divine method of work than this, which directs the everwelling torrents of cosmic energy down through unbroken chains of great Beings and reverent men. To drop one link is impossible. In the occult world it is not permitted to receive the message and to reject the messenger. Nor is it allowable to be ignorant of those universal, self-sustaining laws. Was it not an adept who said: " Ignorance of law cannot be pleaded among men, but ignorance of fact may. In occultism even if you are ignorant of some facts of importance, you are not excused by the Law, for it has regard for no man and pursues its adjustments without regard to what we know or are ignorant of."

The sole question is this. Did H. P. Blavatsky bring us Theosophical revelations from the East or did she not? No one denies that she did. They split up on conventional and personal questions, but not upon this one. Then none of those who have even remotely felt the influence of these revelations, least of all a Society formed and sustained by her, are really in a position to deny her their full support. She does not pay our dues and rental; but are we sustained as a body by those things or by the fresh impetus to occultism and the new ideas given out by her and through her agency and request? Even in the material world some show of gratitude is demanded of us, but in the Eternity it is written, Let all things return through that source whence they proceeded forth. This august law cannot be violated. The Divine working on our plane, must have human agents or vehicles; in private human relations they are human, subject to error.

In all that pertains to their appointed mission they are held to be infallible; if they err there, the consequence falls upon them alone. He who follows the guide appointed to him in the occult order is the gainer by his utter faith and love, even should that guide lead him into error. For his error can soon be set right and is so, while his lack of faith and love cannot be made up for; they are organic defects of the soul.

We are constantly tried upon the question of form versus spirit, as a test of the power of illusion over us. In the Theosophical Society we naturally hold to our rules and laws. These only govern the exoteric body. Thinkers amongst us must long have foreseen the moment these forms must change; a moment when we should be asked to testify to our belief in the esoteric body; that is to say, in the actuality of our Society as a spiritual factor, with spiritual chiefs. We may welcome any such hour of test as a sign of progression on our part. It would set formal laws aside. Well it is, when spirit and letter go together. They are often divorced by the urgencies of this life, and were we not madmen then to choose the letter? New forms grow all too soon, but when the spirit is fled life is lost to that form. We have an opportunity of making such choice when we are asked whether we are ready to endorse H. P. Blavatsky or prefer to stand upon our own independence. That independence is a fancied thing you know. . We are not the natural product of this era, but a graft watered with the heart's blood of one Founder, one out of season in the mere natural order, but permitted, rendered possible, by the eternal order, and constantly invigorated through her. There are those who say, " Surely I can study Theosophy on my own account." Not so, no one can study Divine Wisdom on his own account, or for it. Separation and remoteness are only apparent. We must in thought recognize the sources of our enlightenment and go out in love towards them. Minds and hearts closed to these truths are not open to diviner influence at all. They must recognise that the herald who speaks with trumpet voice to the age alone makes spiritual progress possible to the great mass of men, and each of us must admit and stand ready to pay the debt of Humanity.

I do not consider it in the least necessary for me to know what Madame Blavatsky might do, or even why she does it. I accept the test gladly, as a new step onward, full of joy for my comrades who do so, full of sorrow for those who do not. "Every human action is involved in its faults as the fire in its smoke," says the Gita. Nor does the Lord create those actions or the faculty of acting, we are told, but that "each man's own nature creates them; Nature prevaileth." Every organism thus differentiates the one life according to its progress more or less, while above all the Lord awaits the final evolution of nature into Himself — Itself. Thus it is that her personality and all personalities are beside the question. Here, too, we are tested upon our power to rise above appearances, to look beyond conventions. These shocks are no doubt needed also. So I look to the spirit and to the fixed attitude behind all these various deeds. It is one of generosity, self-abnegation, absolutely fearless devotion to an ideal — the highest ideal known. Each hour of her life is given to the enlightenment of mankind, and such pearls she distributes throughout those weary hours, as might singly ransom the eccentricities of a hundred lives. These personalities are naught. Behind her there is a mystery. She is second to no mere man, and if called to any issue we must choose her from among men and forms; let us hope we shall never be so called, but that all will follow our true Leader.

The Theosophical Society stands to Madame Blavatsky as a child; our life is hers; in and for us she lives. Her great longing is to see us able to stand alone, to have a claim of our own upon the Great Ones; able to draw our own sustenance and strength from the gods before she leaves us. You who know that I have never met her personally, may ask how I may know this. Shall I study the true faithfully and not know that true heart? It is Karma

appoints us our guides through our own attractive influences, and as such H. P. Blavatsky stands to all Theosophists of the century, recorded or unrecorded. We must be prepared to sacrifice some such things as forms, rules, tastes, and opinions, for the sake of truth and occult progress. For such progress an opportunity is now offered us, through the acceptance of a simple test of intuition and faith. For this Madame Blavatsky has my profound and renewed gratitude, and I am, as ever, hers and
Yours faithfully,
JASPER NIEMAND, F.T.S.

FROM *PICCADILLY*, NOVEMBER 2ND, 1888.

MADAME BLAVATSKY is well advanced in years, and physically very infirm, so that she seldom goes beyond her own rooms, but every Saturday afternoon and evening her house is open to all who may be desirous of learning something of those mysteries to which she has devoted her whole life. A Russian by birth, and of good family, Madame Blavatsky was as a child endowed with extraordinary powers of clairvoyance, and, following the guidance of her intuition, she gave her whole energy to the study and development of her higher faculties, and to the source of those mysteries and occult powers which underlie the secret wisdom religion of the ancients. . . . Madame Blavatsky now resides in London, and is engaged in the publication of another stupendous work, entitled *The Secret Doctrine,* a synthesis of science, religion, and philosophy. I found her *chez elle* at Notting Hill, seated at a table covered with green baize, which she presently makes use of as a blackboard for illustrating her discourse. She is smoking a cigarette; so too are many of those (of both sexes) who are listening to her exposition of the knotty questions which have been propounded. The subject under discussion as we enter is the definition of "spirit," and presently growing more eloquent and warm as the questions are pressed further and further back into the regions of the unmanifested, she propounds to us the vast evolution of the soul, the descent of the spirit into matter, and its journey through the manifested universe back to the eternal first cause. Beginning with this first cause—the causeless cause—which is everywhere, yet nowhere; having neither length, breadth, nor height, and represented by a mathematical point, she expounds in Eastern science phraseology the "Days and Nights of Brahmâ," the outbreathing and inbreathing of the spirit by means of which the manifested universe comes into existence. Starting with the mathematical point as the apex of an equilateral triangle, she shows us diagrammatically how the evolution proceeds by the two sides of the triangle (representing wisdom and knowledge); the base line completing the triangle, or Trinity, represents the Logos or Brahma or Osiris or Ormazd, according to which system of philosophy we favour, but which mean the same thing. From this emanate the seven principles called variously the seven Rishis, or the seven Logoi, or the seven Archangels, and from each of these other seven. By this outbreathing of Brahma the manifested worlds came gradually into existence. Everything contains within it a portion or spark of the Divine or Ultimate Consciousness, and it is this spark or ray seeking to return to its source, and to obtain absolute self-consciousness, that evolves through the mineral, vegetable and animal kingdoms. Self-consciousness begins when it reaches the human form, but to obtain absolute consciousness, which is consciousness of everything, it must pass through every form and state of existence, from the highest to the lowest; in other words, it must become the absolute consciousness by experience of everything, which is the absolute consciousness. Seven planes or globes belong to the chain of worlds through which the monad has to evolve, our earth being the fourth in the system to which it belongs, the other planets of this system not being visible to us by reason of their being on another plane of matter. Seven times does the monad journey round this system, tarrying millions of years on each globe, and being incarnated in the human form over and over again, brought back to earth by reason of the desires which were unfulfilled in its past lives and in search of fresh experience, as it ever seeks its way back to its source. How many millions of years all this takes, the duration of each Manvantara, Kalpa, or Yuga, is accurately recorded by those who are the custodians of the knowledge of the Secret Doctrine, which is set forth in mystic form and allegory in many an ancient legend, and in many a sacred book inaccessible to any but those who through many incarnations have resolutely pursued the path that leads to mastership in the occult science. Such is but a brief and imperfect sketch of the eloquent words that fall from the lips of this gifted woman. All listen with eager attention, albeit the strain on the imagination is a severe one. To her it is the A B C of the matter, but when she has somewhat relaxed, we forgive the man who exclaimed, "Ah! our Board Schools have not educated us up to that!"

The conversation now becomes more general, and Madame Blavatsky is asked some question concerning mediumship and spirit manifestations. "Do you know one medium," she asks, "who has made a profession of it and who has not had some serious physical disease, or has not become a drunkard, or a lunatic, or something horrible? What the medium accomplishes is at his or her own expense, it is an expenditure of their vital energy, it is demoralizing both to themselves and to the entities—call them spirits or shells or spooks, or what you will—who seek such persons in order to obtain a temporary vitality. In other cases the phenomena are produced solely by means of what I call a psychological trick, which, however, is not jugglery as commonly understood, but which likewise implies a large expenditure of energy on the part of the medium and can only be done by reserving and storing up the energy; and therefore when you expect a medium to give many séances a day, for which he is paid his guinea, or whatever it may be, you simply expect him to do that which he could not perform with his vital powers—in fact you simply pay to be cheated. Hundreds of persons have heard the astral bell and raps which I used to perform at will, but which if I were to attempt now would probably be fatal by reason of the weakness of my heart. I have made one gentleman (a leading scientific man) produce the 'astral bells' himself, while I simply touched him with my fingers, he, meanwhile, concentrating his mind on the phenomenon to be produced. He did not always succeed, because it requires long practice to do it at will, but I proved to him that it was nothing more than a manifestation of will power through psychological faculties which are not known to men of science, or are but partially acknowledged in the form of mesmerism or thought transference. For instance, many people have this power in the form of a magnetic or healing touch; this I never had, but I could produce various phenomena with inanimate matter. In New York I was given a test which created a great sensation at the time. A sheet of clean note paper was brought to me from a certain club-room, having the heading of the club stamped on it. I laid my hand on the paper, and concentrating my mind on the features of an Eastern Yogi, with whose physiognomy I was intimately acquainted, I presently removed my hand, and there was seen the portrait of the man on whom I had concentrated my thoughts and then projected on the paper by means of my will power. This portrait was examined by some of the leading artists in New York, and in sworn evidence they said that it was impossible for them to tell by what means the portrait was impressed on the paper; it was not done by any of the processes with which they, as experts, were familiar, and, moreover, with regard to the artistic qualities of the representation, it was such as could only have been produced by the greatest master in the art of portraiture who had ever lived. Science, so-called, does not know anything about these powers of the will, but they have been known to occultists for ages, and many more things which have been set down as magic or miracle. The portrait is still in the possession of Col. Olcott, and you will find a full account of the circumstances, and the names of the artists and other gentlemen who witnessed it, in the book which has recently been published under the title of *Incidents in the Life of Madame Blavatsky*.

"Will not these powers and faculties," I ask, "presently become the common property of the race?"

"Most certainly," replies Madame Blavatsky. "The race as a whole progresses, but many individuals outstrip their fellows; clairvoyance, mesmerism, psychometry, and many other little understood matters, are the beginning of faculties which are now exercised by many individuals in a partial degree, and more or less unconsciously. The aim of the occultist is to develope those powers to the full, and to exercise them consciously for the good of humanity. The Mahâtmâs, or Adepts, who are the custodians of the knowledge of the occult powers of nature, are men who have acquired these faculties by long and arduous efforts in past incarnations. By reason of these powers they are able to study nature on a higher plane than that of our physical senses, and, therefore, what, to the ordinary individual, must be a matter of faith, is to them a matter of experience and knowledge. It is some portion of their knowledge which I have gained from them, and which I am now permitted to give to the world."

I could have stayed much longer listening to the discourse of this remarkable woman, but it was drawing towards midnight, and, mindful of the infirmities of our hostess, I rose to go. She bade me adieu with a warm invitation to come again, and, as I stepped into the outer world, I felt that there were indeed more things in heaven and earth than either our science or our philosophy conceives of, and that if we are unable to penetrate those mysteries for ourselves, we might, at least, look to those who had done so for higher and broader ideas with respect to the destiny of the race and of the individual.

FROM *NEW YORK TIMES*, JANUARY 6th, 1889.

"Madame Blavatsky," said Mr. Judge, in a conversation since his return (from London), "is living with the Countess Wachtmeister—widow of a Swedish Count, who was Norwegian and Swedish Minister to the Court of St. James'—in Holland Park, London, and is devoting herself to the most arduous labour in the cause of Theosophy. She scarcely ever leaves the house, and from 6.30 in the morning until the evening is constantly engaged in writing articles for her magazine *Lucifer*, or other Theosophical publications, replying to correspondents, and preparing the matter for the further forthcoming volumes of her gigantic work *The Secret Doctrine*. In the evening she has many visitors of all sorts—enquirers, critics, sceptics, curiosity-seekers, friends—and all are welcomed with such charming grace, friendliness and simplicity that every one is made to feel at home with her. By ten o'clock generally all but intimate friends have retired, but they remain an hour or two later.

"Notwithstanding that Madame Blavatsky is beyond the vigour of middle age, and for nearly three weeks past has been living in spite of the leading London physicians, who gave her up long ago as hopelessly incurable of a deadly kidney disease that was liable to kill her at any moment, she never seems weary, but is the animated leader of conversation, speaking with equal ease in English, French, Italian and Russian, or dropping into Hindoostanee as occasion requires. Whether working or talking, she seems to be constantly rolling, lighting and smoking cigarettes of Turkish tobacco. As for her personal appearance, she hardly seems changed at all from what she was when in this country several years ago, except that she has grown somewhat stouter. The characteristics that are most apparent in her countenance are, in equal blending, energy and great kindness. Looking at her one can realise that she is just the sort of woman who would do what she did a dozen years ago when she was coming over here from France. She reached Havre with a first class ticket to New York, and only two or three dollars over, for she never carried much money. Just as she was going aboard the steamer, she saw a poor woman, accompanied by two little children, who was sitting on the pier, weeping bitterly.

"'Why are you crying?' she asked.

"The woman replied that her husband had sent to her from America money to enable her and the children to join him. She had expended it all in the purchase of steerage tickets for herself that turned out to be utterly valueless counterfeits. Where to find the swindler who had so heartlessly defrauded her she did not know, and she was quite penniless in a strange city. 'Come with me,' said Madame Blavatsky, who straightway went to the agent of the steamship company and induced him to exchange her first class ticket for steerage tickets for herself, the poor woman and the children. Anybody who has ever crossed the ocean in the steerage among a crowd of emigrants will appreciate the magnitude of such a sacrifice to a woman of fine sensibilities, and there are few but Madame Blavatsky who would have been capable of it.

"As I said, she has been condemned to death for three years, but no fear is entertained of her dying before her mission is accomplished. Twice before when in India she was given up by the doctors, who on each occasion set a time limit of only a few days upon her existence, and her recoveries were looked upon as simply marvellous. At the time when she was worst, and seemed likely to die on the road, she set out for Northern India, and as it was generally understood that she was going to the Mahâtmâs for succour, several persons who had a strong desire to see those mysterious Adepts followed and watched her, but at Dharjeeling she mysteriously disappeared. She had been carried there, and it was inconceivable how she could by herself have slipped away, but she was gone, and that was all anybody could say about it. In three days she returned apparently as well as she ever was. The most that anyone is told about how the transformation in her condition was effected, is given by her in *The Secret Doctrine*, when she says:—

"'Sound generates or rather attracts together the elements that produce an ozone, the fabrication of which is beyond chemistry but within the limits of alchemy. It may even resurrect a man or an animal whose astral 'vital body' has not been irreparably separated from the physical body by the severance of the magnetic or odic body. As one thrice raised from death by that power the writer ought to be credited with knowing personally something about it."

'Madame Blavatsky now very seldom gives any manifestation of her occult powers except to intimate friends; but I had while over there several evidences that she can do things quite inexplicable by any laws of exact science. Two years ago I lost here in New York a paper that was of considerable interest to me.

"I do not think anybody but myself knew that I had it,

and I certainly mentioned to no one that I had lost it. One evening a little over a fortnight ago, while I was sitting in Madame Blavatsky's parlour with Mr. B. Keightley and several other persons, I happened to think of that paper. Madame got up, went into the next room, and, returning, almost immediately handed to me a sheet of paper. I opened it and found it an exact duplicate of the paper that I had lost two years before. It was actually a facsimile copy, as I recognised at once. I thanked her, and she said:

"'Well, I saw it in your head that you wanted it.'

"It was not a thing to astonish anyone acquainted with the laws of nature as comprehended by occultists, who understand clearly how consciousness of my thought was possible, how the reproduction of a thing once within my knowledge was necessarily facsimile, and how that reproduction could be effected by a simple act of volition on her part, but it would puzzle materialists to explain it in accordance with the facts.

"One night when I talked very late with a gentleman at a house distant from Madame Blavatsky's, he expressed a wish that I would, if I had an opportunity, get her views, without mentioning his name, upon a subject that was under discussion between us. The next day when I was talking with her the subject came up, and I began offering his suggestion, when she interrupted me, saying:

"'You need not tell me that; I was there last night and heard you,' and went on to repeat all that had been said Of course it can be said that he had informed her with a view to deceiving me, but I am well assured that there was nothing of the sort and that under certain existing circumstances that would have been practically impossible. I know that she very often reads people's thoughts and replies to them in words.

"The silvery bell sounds in the astral current that were heard over her head by so many persons in New York, still continue to follow her, and it is beyond question to those familiar with her life and work that she is in constant receipt of the most potent aid from the adepts, particularly her teacher, the ——— whose portrait hangs in her study and shows a dark and beautiful Indian face, full of sweetness, wisdom and majesty. Of course it does not seem possible that he in Tibet instantaneously responds either by a mental impression or a "precipitated" note to a mental interrogatory put to her in London, but it happens to be a fact that he does so all the same."

FROM THE LONDON *STAR*, DEC. 18TH, 1888.

THERE are nearly as many Madame Blavatskys as you please. There is, for example, the Madame Blavatsky of the Psychical Research Society, which, if I remember rightly, has in one of its oracular reports assigned her a distinguished place on the roll of the world's impostors. There is the Madame Blavatsky of popular repute and report, who looks large and uncertain. *Monstrum informe ingens horrendum* in the imagination of Europe—a sort of female Cagliostro, or wonder worker, who is wafted through stone walls like Mrs. Guppy, and bodily up into the heavens like the just Enoch.

There is then the Madame Blavatsky (known to the Brotherhood as H. P. B.) of her own Theosophical Society, the members of which look upon her as a searcher after and teacher of truths not known to, or not understood of the many, as the foremost exponent (in Europe at any rate) of the so-called occult science, and as a depository in some measure of that so-called *Secret Doctrine* which is supposed to contain the essential veracities of all the religions and philosophies that are or ever were.

Once more there is the Madame Blavatsky whom strangers from the outer darkness are permitted to see at her house in Holland Park, and to whom she reveals herself as a lady of exceptional charm of manner, wonderful variety of information, and powers of conversation which recall the giant talkers of a bygone literary age.

"It was as one from the outer darkness," says a *Star* man, "that I visited her a day or so ago. I had a delightfully humorous little note in my pocket, inviting me to tea, and warning me that I should find the writer 'as easy to interview as a sacred crocodile of old Nile.' The envelope of this note bore a mystic symbol, and the unimpeachable motto that there is no religion higher than truth.

"I was led into a little snug room on the ground floor of a substantial house, where two lamps and a gas stove glowed like a triple star. I smelt Turkish tobacco strongly, and behind the red disk of a cigarette I saw the broad and impressive countenance of Madame Blavatsky. Short and redundant, and swathed rather than fitted in black silk, she is a very remarkable figure. The dark almost swarthy face looks a little heavy at first (my immediate impression was of a feminine reincarnation of Cagliostro), with its wide nostrils, large soft eyes, and full and weighty lips. But by and by it shows itself a mobile and expressive face, very sympathetic and very intellectual. And whilst on this gross subject of personal description (a liberty for which the interviewer should always apologise sincerely to the interviewed) let me note the delicate plumpness of the hands.

"A circular box of carved wood at her elbow furnishes Madame Blavatsky with the tobacco for the cigarettes which she smokes incessantly, from six in the morning, when she commences work, until she puts out her lamp for the night. Besides the tobacco box, there is only one other notable object in her sanctum, the portrait of the Mahâtmâ Morya (a descendant, she says, of the old dynasty of the Moryas), whom she calls her Master, a dark and beautiful Indian face, full of sweetness and wisdom. This seer Madame Blavatsky has seen, she says, at various times in the flesh: in England once, in India on many occasions, and some years ago she went to seek him in the fastnesses of Tibet, a romantic pilgrimage by no means free from peril, during which she penetrated some of the Buddhist monasteries or Lamaseries, and had converse with the recluses there. But Madame Blavatsky's disciples have many stories to tell of the extraordinary way in which her Mahâtmâ communicates with her. Letters that never paid postage, nor passed through St. Martin's-le-Grand, are seen to flutter down into her lap. Literary quotations that she is sometimes bothered to find are put into her hand written out upon strips of paper. The manuscript that she leaves on her desk over night is often found by her in the morning with passages corrected, expunged, or re-written, marginal notes inserted, and so on, in the handwriting of the Mahâtmâ Morya.

"Sufficiently surprising too, are the powers with which her Theosóphical associates credit Madame herself. Those who live with her in Lansdowne Road see wonders daily, and have left off being surprised. Once accept the theory that the psychic faculties latent within us are capable, under certain conditions, of being developed to any extent, and magical doings of all sorts become easy of credence, and belief in what is called the astral is, I believe, a cardinal article of belief with the Theosophists. Here is a funny little circumstance that one of the Blavatsky household—an intelligent American gentleman—related gravely and in evident good faith. Madame Blavatsky rolled a cigarette and was going to light it, but found that her matchbox was empty. Over her head was a swinging lamp, so high that she could not have reached it had she mounted on her chair to do so. The American gentleman, who was sitting with her at the time, declares that he saw her gradually elongate herself—so it appeared to him—until she could lean over the lamp, when she lighted her cigarette, then sank back in her chair and resumed her writing. But these phenomena are not witnessed by everybody, and perhaps I need scarcely add that Madame Blavatsky (though freely offering me the contents of her tobacco box) declined to work a miracle for me. Doubtless her refusal was wise, for if I had seen one of these uncanny sights with my own eyes, which of you would have believed my report of it?

" We talked of many things.

" ' What is Theosophy, Madame ? ' I asked. 'Do you call it a religion ?

" ' Most distinctly not,' she replied, ' there are too many religions in the world already. I don't propose to add to the number.'

" ' What, may I ask, is the Theosophical attitude towards these too numerous religions ? '

"Madame Blavatsky thereupon entered upon a long and interesting explanation on this subject, from which I gathered that Theosophy looks upon all religions as good in one sense, and all religions as bad in another sense. There are truths underlying all, and there are falsities *overlying* all. Most faiths are good at the core, all are more or less wrong in their external manifestations; and all the trappings of religions, all their shows and ceremonies, are entirely repudiated by the Theosophists. The conditions under which aspirants become members of the Theosophical Society are few and simple. Merely to join the Society it is sufficient to profess oneself in sympathy with its objects, of which there are three in chief—the promotion of a universal brotherhood amongst men, the study of religions, and the development of the psychic faculties latent in man. The last-named object is for the attainment of advanced members, who have gained admittance to the esoteric section of the society. It is only in the esoteric section for example that you can expect to learn how to elongate yourself.

"Madame herself, in her vigorous intellectual way, is quite as dogmatic as the most dogmatic professor of what (under Theosophical favour) are called the exact sciences; and, indeed, dogmatism, both in affirmation and denial, seems the badge of all the Theosophical tribe. . . . It was seven o'clock before Madame Blavatsky had exhausted my interest, or I, as I hoped, her patience; and at seven the members of the household assembled for dinner.

"The household consists of six or seven persons, including a young doctor of medicine, a student of law and a Frenchman, an American (the friend of Edison who was mentioned in the *Star* the other day), and a Swedish

Countess. These are all particular disciples, who receive constant instructions from the lips of the priestess, and who may be regarded as well on the way towards the attainment of the elongating principle. The flourishing prospects of Madame's new work, *The Secret Doctrine*, the first edition of which is already disposed of, though the volumes are scarcely out of the printer's hands, were discussed during the meal. Madame's years—she is bordering on the sixties—and her occasional difficulties with the language—she is a Russian by birth—do not prevent her from being the most energetic and entertaining talker at her table.

"It was the evening on which the Blavatsky Lodge holds its weekly meeting, and by half-past eight the sanctum, whither we adjourned after dinner, was filled with a little gathering of would-be elongators of both sexes. The subject for discussion was dreams. The circular tobacco box having been replenished by Madame's little maid, and the president in evening dress having taken his place by Madame's side, the secretary of the lodge began to ask questions from a paper."

SUNDAY TRIBUNE, MAY 18TH, 1890.

Madame Blavatsky.

A TALK with her familiar friend and private secretary, Mr. Bertram Keightley, did not disappoint the expectant interviewer who sought him out during his recent visit to this city. Of himself he said, "I have been interested in Theosophy since 1884, when I first met Madame Blavatsky and Colonel Olcott. At that time I became quite well acquainted with them, for I spent some time with Madame in Germany, and afterwards with Col. Olcott in England. That visit in Germany with a party of friends was afterwards written up in story form by Mr. A. P. Sinnett, under the name of *Karma*. Mr. Sinnett was one of the guests. In the Baron, of course, you will recognise Madame Blavatsky. . . I had been prepared to accept Theosophy by a previous study of mysticism, to which I was led by an experimental study of mesmerism. I was working with disconnected clues until I got hold of Theosophy, and then I realised at once that I had found the whole of which I had before received only parts. My nephew, Archibald Keightley, who is nearly my own age, and who has like me devoted himself to the cause of Theosophy, became interested shortly afterwards.

"It was in 1887 that, at my request, Madame Blavatsky went to England to live, accompanied by the Countess Wachtmeister, the widow of a former ambassador to the English Court.

"Since that time we have been members of one household, and the Countess has taken charge of the house. Our family is a somewhat numerous one, including, besides those already mentioned and Archibald Keightley, several other active workers in the cause.

"Madame Blavatsky occupies rooms on the ground floor, the large drawing-room serving for her working-room, out of which her sleeping apartment opens. Folding doors connect the drawing-room with our dining-room, where we all dine together, and where she generally joins us. During the day she sits at a desk in the bay window, working generally from 7.30 in the morning to 7 in the evening, She works constantly, not once in three months going out of those three rooms. She sits in a large armchair with a long desk on one side and a table on the other, making a kind of box around her.

"Thursday evening when the lodge meets she turns her chair about and sits facing the company. Everybody asks questions, which she answers with great patience whenever she sees an earnest desire to learn. Often persons who are not Theosophists go to her for information, and they are always received with extreme kindness when they show the same earnestness. She will then never say a word that will wound their feelings or their belief, whatever it may be, but one of her marked traits is a positive detestation of shams. She simply won't stand that sort of thing, and if people go to her flippantly or with cant she is pretty sure to cut them all to pieces, and, metaphorically speaking, scatter them over the room.

"In personal appearance Madame Blavatsky is of medium height, but so stout that she appears shorter than she really is. She has rich dark-brown hair that lies in waves all over her head. Her eyes are bright gray and most peculiar, seeming to look right through a person, and they do too," added Mr. Keightley with a smile. "Her complexion is a clear olive. She has beautiful hands, delicate and so flexible that they bend backwards with ease, her finger tips all curl backwards in the prettiest way imaginable. The main characteristic of her face I would say, is its immense force, its intellectuality. She is truly magnificent in this, and her energy is wholly phenomenal. I have seen her after a day's work so tired that she looked positively ill and quite unfit for any further exertion, but if need arose, if fresh work was to be done, or some theosophical question came up for discussion, she seemed to renew her strength with the desire, and would plunge into whatever offered with a resistless energy as if she had never known weariness. Usually in the evening she sits at a small centre table playing 'patience' or some other game of cards, while talking all the time about Theosophy, symbolisms, religions, and other metaphysical questions. The solitary game she plays serves simply as a slight diversion for a mind continually occupied with profound thoughts."

FROM *THE COMMERCIAL GAZETTE.*

CINCINNATI, SUNDAY, OCTOBER 13TH, 1889.

A VISIT TO MADAME BLAVATSKY.

SINCE the time, many years ago, when the daily papers told us of a mysterious and gifted woman in our midst, who was preparing a book of occult lore, such as had never before been given to the readers of our western world, up to the present time, when the author of *Isis Unveiled* is recognized in the literary world as one of its indefatigable workers, in the religious world as an enemy to old beliefs, and in the social world as a woman as incomprehensible as a sphinx—Madame Blavatsky is without doubt the most remarkable woman of the age. Shrug your shoulders, my friend, and utter the word infamous if you choose, but you will find it no easy task to prove aught that will derogate from her character or ability, and no one will venture to assert that any other woman is known around the world like her. It matters little who the reader may be, judge, clergyman or professor, every item regarding the life of this lady is read with interest. One is told that she is five hundred years old and renews her age in the far east as often as it is necessary; another tells of magical feats where crisp new bills are improvised by a moment's thought, or as Lytton calls it, by will power; a third affirms that she has been exposed as a cheat and a trickster, and so on *ad infinitum*.

While all the world read and discuss, she lives and writes, and performs an amount of literary work as astonishing in its amount as in its subject matter. A few days ago it was the writer's good fortune to call upon Madame Blavatsky at her home in London. The day was rainy, as London days always are, and the drive from Charing Cross to Holland Park in a two-wheeled cab would have been anything but agreeable, had not the mind for a time forgotten the body and busied itself with memories of the long years of patient waiting since first the desire to see her had taken possession of it. Pilgrims to Mecca, the devout who at length have audience with the Pope, the American who gains the privilege of a presentation at court, the tourist who sees Mont Blanc for the first time, all these sink into insignificance before the experience of emotions in which all these are blended, and a something added which mystery alone gives, as one wheels along the crowded London thoroughfares on a visit to Madame Blavatsky.

The rain increases every moment, and after twenty minutes' hard driving the cabman stops at No. 7, Lansdowne Road. It no longer rains, it pours, and the pilgrim dashes through the falling torrents to find that the number is not 7, but 17. With thanks for the information and the mental comment that the lady in question must be well known, another dash through the rain is made and the number is sought. Lansdowne Road is one of those wide, beautiful streets that are to be found in the neighbourhood of Hyde Park, where every house is a home, and a home that might satisfy nobility. Well kept gardens or yards of green shrubbery add a charm to the substantial stone buildings that are here the fashion. "Oui, Madame, entrez, s'il vous plait," was the cordial response to the question, "Is Madame Blavatsky in, and can I see her?"

Ushered into the first room to the left, wherein a large table and furniture betoken use,—perhaps as a dining room, perhaps as a reception room, and sometimes as a study, for upon the table were divers papers and writings—I waited for further orders. A few moments later the folding doors were thrown open and I stood face to face with a gentleman of grand physique, of genial face, of wonderful beard, a gentleman so unique in manner and appearance that I at once involuntarily exclaimed: "Colonel Olcott."

"The same, and you are my countrywoman. Be seated." He had only arrived in London from India a few days before, and the minutes flew as he spoke of the work, and was only interrupted by a door opening, announcing the entrance of Madame Blavatsky. How shall I describe her? It would be impossible. A general impression of kindliness, of power, of wonderful gifts, is all that remains at this moment on my mind. She moved with difficulty, for she was suffering greatly from rheumatism, but she laughingly asserted, as she seated herself in an easy chair, "I have cheated the doctors and death so many times before they say, that I hope to cheat this rheumatism also, but it is not so easy to manage."

"But you still write, Madame?"

"Of course, I write as much as ever;" and Colonel Olcott interrupted with, " What matters about a little rheumatism so long as it does not creep into her head or her writings?" And we all laughed. When I said, " *Lucifer* is quite at home in America," she replied with spirit, " They have boycotted it in London, and will not allow it to be sold at the news-stands." I could scarcely comprehend this and she laughed as she said : " There are people who believe I am the devil with horns and hoofs," and again we laughed.

We talked of Theosophy and its rapid spread, its workers and writers, and of Dr. Buck, of Cincinnati, whose picture hung just above my head, where his well-known face seemed to smile a welcome to us all. "Have you seen this work noticed, Madame?" and she laid in my hand the advanced sheets of her new book, *The Key to Theosophy*. I had not, and she said it would be issued very soon, also a smaller work she had just finished, *The Voice of the Silence*. When I expressed surprise at the amount of writing she had done, as well as the immense knowledge displayed, Colonel Olcott remarked: "I worked with Madame Blavatsky for several years and know all about it. She is a steam engine at writing, and when I tell you that in writing *Isis Unveiled*, with its large number of extracts from ancient writings, she had access but to a small bookcase of ordinary books, you will believe me when I tell you that she reads as clearly in the astral light as from the open pages." All this time I was conscious of a pair of eyes that were reading my very thoughts, and a face opposite me that might become at any moment as immovable as the sphinx, but was very kindly and animated at the present moment ; I can imagine no personality so expressive of indomitable will power as Madame Blavatsky.

The room in which we sat was instinct with her individuality. It was full of everything that suggested thought, refinement, literary labour, an interest in friends, but there was no place for mere display of useless ornament. The table, with Colonel Olcott on one side and herself on the other, was loaded with papers and books, the walls were covered with photographs; and here in the heart of the bustling city lives and works the founder of the Theosophical Society, that now numbers in America alone more than thirty branches. All this has been accomplished in little over a decade.

www.ingramcontent.com/pod-product-compliance
Lightning Source LLC
Chambersburg PA
CBHW030311170426
43202CB00009B/959